T0132159

Justice

FOR THE

Mentally Challenged

JEREMIAH RUSSELL

iUniverse, Inc.
Bloomington

Justice for the Mentally Challenged

iUniverse books may be ordered through booksellers or by contacting:

iUniverse
1663 Liberty Drive
Bloomington, IN 47403
www.iuniverse.com
1-800-Authors (1-800-288-4677)

ISBN: 978-1-4620-1065-3 (pbk)
ISBN: 978-1-4620-1114-8 (ebk)

Printed in the United States of America

iUniverse rev. date: 4/5/11

Introduction

This book is about justice to someone who is mentally challenged. This book is about my experiences with mental health medications, and the justice system while under those drugs. These stories are true from court records, but the names are changed, because the court can be unfair at times, and I want to make sure that my story can be told without the court saying it can't.

I'm also working on a daily dairy of things on my mind that I will add in this book, so the reader can take a look inside my mind and life. These stories of the justice system I'm bring you will show things about me that I'm not proud of , but willing to show you my mistakes in life and how they were handled.

I have come a long way from the hell of prison cells and the reader can learn how I got there and what happen in the court as I pleaded my case. Some times in court I was so heavily drugged that I couldn't even see straight. I have been to prison twice and both times I received a stiff sentence , the first time was for receiving stolen property, and the second time was threaten the President which I talked about why, and how that happened in my first book that I hope you have read called "Insanity"

The book will show how I was done. Many people take advantage of people going through a mental crisis; some people have mental break downs, in the free world and even more behind bars. Prison was the hardest thing to deal with mentally. I hope you enjoy this interesting book and see my side of the coin. I have been angry at the injustice for what has taken place in the court for a long time, but I have peace about it now. I tell this story, and in a way that you will know all the facts, when the court made its judgments I know they didn't have all the facts, and a lot was said that was untrue.

Thanks for reviewing this book, hope you in joy it. I want to thank the publisher for make my dreams come true to have my story out there for you to read and hope you learn a few things that you may not have known. I also want to say thanks to God, I'm doing great, and all the hard things I've lived through has made me stronger. God bless our country and maybe if a few judges read this then maybe they will see how things can go in the court room.

Best Wishes,

Jeremiah Russell

= Chapter 1 =

When I was 19 years old I rode a stolen motor cycle and charged with receiving stolen property. What happens is my friend found the key at my apartment complex in the laundry room. He said the key fits a motor cycle, and the complex had a place where people parked their bikes. So we went up to the bikes and there was a brand new crotch rocket there that the key fit, we crank it up. I went back to my apartment and began drinking. I never intended to still the bike. As I got drunk later in the day, it had turned into night time. I wanted to ride the motor cycle so I went back to the bikes and cranked it up again. I had barrowed a helmet from a guy that lived next door.

As I was drunk and got on the bike, I saw where it said the bike could go if I remember right 180 miles an hour, if not faster. It was a really nice bike. My plans where to just drive it then park it back, and that is what happen, I wreck it before I parked it back. What happen was when I got on it to ride it I had in it in the parking lot complex and it went from zero to 80 miles per hour within just seconds. I couldn't find the brake with my foot, so I used the brake on the handle bars, which was the front brake. The bike started sliding out from under me, and I slide across the payment with me leg trapped under it. I had wrecked the motor cycle right in front of my apartment. My legs were hurt, it felt like it was broke, but I was able to pick up the bike because I was drunk. The pain hurt really bad, but I was also in fear, because it wasn't my bike.

I put the bike back into its parking spot, I had pushed it about a foot ball felid length, hurt. The bike only had a few scratches, but I was

1

hurt. I went back to my apartment and passed out, I woke up with the sheets stuck to my wounded legs, I ripped the sheet off as it has stuck to my flesh, I had a friend take me to the hospital because I could not drive.

You could tell that the bike was wreck right in front of where I lived. A few nights later I had a few friends over and I was drunk again on pain pills as well, I got a knock on the door and it was a girl, she asked has anyone seen someone wreck a motor cycle outside, she saw I was hurt and ask me what happen to me, I told her I wrecked my dirt bike, because at the time I had a dirt bike. She said someone wrecked her boy friends motor cycle. Well about an hour later the law knocked on my door, they had stopped my friends who had just left and asked them about my wound. Well the cop asked me about how I wrecked, and said he talked to my friends who said I wrecked the stolen motor cycle.

I gave him this story that someone tried selling me the bike and I was test driving it, it was a story from a drunk fool, the cop said he couldn't take me to jail, but the guy could go get a warrant, and that is what happen, the guy went and got a warrant at the court house. The next day I was in jail.

I got bonded out and waiting for a court date, well someone happen and I missed my court date, so I was back in jail without a bond. I plead guilty to receiving stolen property and got 7 years probation. Well I moved to Florida and never reported to probation. As you will learn later I got into trouble in Florida and they didn't send me back to Ga. Four years later I was arrested in Ga. , as I was in the jail it was hard on me, there where 70 guys to a dorm and the lights stayed on all night and people talking all night, so I ask to see the doctor, I wanted sleeping medication and the only way I could get it was to say I was suicidal. I didn't know what I was getting into with this doctor. He gave me meds that where not only help me sleep but harming me, so I tried other meds and learned most of the meds have a lot of side effects. Then I said I was just going to stop taking the meds because the side effects where really messing with my head, it was causing mental health problems, messing with my nerves system and much more. So the doctor told me that if I would take the meds he was going to put me in lock up, and that is what he did. It was a padded cell with no bed, the floor was padded as well, the air was on cold and I had a paper gown on, it tore apart in about five minutes. Now I was in the crazy cell feeling crazy because the meds had my mind tripped out. The doctor took a vacation for about four days. I was so cold and didn't have a blanket or anything, I was freezing. When the doctor came back he said the only way I could get out of that cold cell was to take the meds he ordered, which had bad side effects, but I was wanting out because it was torture.

When I went to court I was sentenced to prison, you will find out in the pages to come how I was done by not just the court but the public defender as well. I had trouble after taking the meds and every time I stopped taking them I got more scrootnee. My life in prison was a nightmare, but I started going to the law library and trying to get back into court and you will learn why and what happen. I really had know chance but to just plead my case. You will see what I had to say and why.

I filled a Writ of Habeas Corpus and had a hearing on my complaint. What your about to read is the hearing that took place, I changed the names to a color code just to not have others come back with a law suit or anything like that. I am no lawyer but it clear I made my point. I did not win the hearing but I was able to tell my side of injustice, and now can share it with you . I cant go back in time and change anything, but this forever took place, and it happens more than people may know.

After you read this hearing later on in the book I will share with you more of things that took place as I see it as an injustice in my life, in a whole new case. Here is the Habeas Corpus Hearing, remember a Habeas Corpus Hearing is the highest hearing in the land. And this took place while I was under mental health care, I received drugs my whole prison term that caused many side effects.

= Chapter 2 =

In The Superior Court

JEREMIAH RUSSELL,

WRIT OF HABEAS CORPUS HEARING

PETITIONER

#5 Motion Docket,

V,

May 28, XXXX

RESPONDENTS

The proceedings of the WRIT OF HABEAS CORPUS Hearing of the within captioned case held at the above stated time and place before the Honorable Judge.

Appearances of Document

The Court: This is the case of Jeremiah Russell, verses XXXXXXXXX, Habeas Corpus. Are you Mr. Russell?

The Petitioner: Yes sir.

The Court: Are you ready to proceed?

The Petitioner: Yes sir.

The Court: You are Mr. Blue?

Mr. Blue: Yes, Your Honor

The Court: You are representing…

Mr. Blue: On behalf of the Warden we are ready to Proceed also.

The Court: All right

Mr: Blue: We will call as our first witness the Petitioner's trail attorney. Judge, by way of background This case arose in trail court of XXXX County Superior Court. In XXXX, on October the 12th, the Petitioner pled And in connection with this plea, one count of theft by Taking was offered for nolle prosequi. He was represented by counsel at that proceeding. He received a 7 year probated sentence for that offense in XXXX. Following his convictions for various offenses in the State of Florida, later then in Georgia, in October of XXXX, the Petitioner's probation was revoked in part. He received – 3 years of his 7 year sentence was revoked; he did spend a period of time in pre-trail confinement prior to the entry of the Revocation Order. He did not appeal – did not pursue any Administrative remedies or attempt to appeal his revocation Proceedings. The Petitioner's claim are that his revocation Plea – I'll call it – was improperly induced, that he Thought he would get credit for a certain period of time That he had served prior to the entry of the Revocation Order. And he alleges that his trail counsel misled him with respect to his receiving time served. So we have counsel here, his name is Mr. Red, and we are prepared to have him sworn and offer testimony. Court: All right. What do you want to say, Mr. Russell?

The Petitioner: Sir, I have a few cases here that I sent in on my brief that I would like to underline. The first one is Smith versus State: The burden of proof of waiver – the burden rest upon the State to demonstrate clearly that the defendant knowingly and intelligently waived his privilege against self-incrimination. I was on, at the time, psychotropic medication, Stelazine and Zyprexa, and I was having many side effects, and one of them was blurred vision. And the next case that I would like to underline is Cooper versus Griffen: Factors bearing on waiver of Constitutional rights and mental deficiency. I've been treated several times since being locked up.

The Court: What kind of mental deficiency?

The Petitioner: I can call my counselor, Mr. Green, to tell you my diagnosis. At the time I was on heavy medications; I didn't get a competency hearing...

The Court: That's not what I asked. What is your mental deficiency?

The Petitioner: I things like state of depression and I'm very spiritual.

The Court: How far did you go in school?

The Petitioner: I got a G. E. D when I was 16 years old.

The Court: When you where 16?

The Petitioner: Yes sir.

The Court: What type of work do you do?

The Petitioner: A painter.

The Court: All right.

The Petitioner: But at the time, just to days prior to going to go to court my dosage of medicine was changed at the County Jail – just two days prior to going to court. The next case I would like to underline is Walker versus Caldwell – But significant misleading statements of counsel can rise to a level of denial of due process of law and result in violation of judicial proceeding and ineffective assistance of counsel. Mr. Red my public defender told me the day I went to court that I would get credit for time served, which was 8 months prior to going to court. On the first court date he didn't even show up and they off – set it a month that I didn't get credit for that time. The second court date the judge had to get the Clerk to call him to come up there. And I would like to underline Bridwell versus Aderhold – failure to make effective appointment violates U. S. Constitutional Amendments V and XIV. The necessity of counsel is so vital and imperative that the failure of trail court to make an effective appointment of counsel is likewise a denial of dew process within the meaning of the U. S. Constitutional Amendments V and XIV.

The Court: Let me see – you were placed on probation in the year of XXXX…

The Petitioner: Yes sir.

The Court: What were the terms of your probation?

The Petitioner: I don't have that information.

The Court: You weren't told that you had to report to the probation officer—that you had to remain steadily employed; report to the probation officer once a month?

The Petitioner: Yes sir.

The Court: Were you required to pay a fine?

The petitioner: Yes sir.

The Court: How much?

The Petitioner; I'm not sure; I don't have that Information.

The Court: How much did you pay on your fine?

The Petitioner: I paid—my mother had moved to Sarasota, Florida, and my step dad got a blood clot in his brain, and my mom wanted me to help them to pay their bills, and they wouldn't transfer my probation, so I left out on probation.

The Court: So you left and did not report to the Probation officer?

The Petitioner: Yes sir.

The Court: When was the last time that you reported?

= CHAPTER 3 =

The petitioner: XXXX

The Court: So you don't report any for...

The Petitioner: For four years.

The Court: After you were sentenced...

The Petitioner: Yes sir.

The Court: So you didn't report any?

The Petitioner: Yes sir.

The Court So you just went to Florida and stayed down There?

The Petitioner: Sir...

The Court: I'm just asking; I don't know.

The Petitioner: Yes air. I know on my probation revocation...

The Court: Did you get arrested in Florida?

The Petitioner: Yes sir.

The Court: What for?

The Petitioner: Resisting arrest and powder cocaine.

The Court: What happened to that case?

The Petitioner: They gave me 7 months.

The Court: So you were convicted in Florida...

The petitioner: Yes sir.

The Court: ..... for violating the law?

The Petitioner: Your Honor, I would like to withdraw my guilty plea on the fact that I was on heavy medication the day I was in court.

The Court: Which day ar you talking about now?

The Petitioner: October 12, XXXX, my revocation hearing. I would like to have a new revocation hearing, because the charges on the revocation—I'm not guilty of the charges on the revocation. I was not able to read at the time because I was on heavy medications.

The Court: Were you found guilty in Florida?

The Petitioner: Yes sir.

The Court: So there was a record that you were found guilty?

 The Petitioner: I'm not saying I'm not guilty of some of the charges...

The Court: I'm trying to find out. They had you for absconding supervision, not reporting to the probation officer, and so forth, and, I assume, that you had been found guilty in Florida for a new offense.

The Petitioner: Exactly, but they...

The Court: Now I'm interested to find out what you expected your lawyer to do under those circumstances.

 The Petitioner: He had explained to me...

The Court: No- what did you expect him to do. That's What I'm asking you.

The Petitioner: At that time what did I expect him to do?

The Court: Yes.

The Petitioner: Give me a reasonable counsel, not to lie to me.

The Court: What would you expect him to do under those circumstances? What defense did you have? That's what I'm trying to find out.

The Petitioner: Well, on the revocation, those charges That I'm not guilty of...

The Court: You didn't abscond supervision>

The Petition: I'm not saying some of the charges I was not guilty of, but there are some charges on there that I'm not guilty of. On May 3rd—he had told me that it was going to be a two year revocation to serve in the probation detention center, when it was a three year prison sentence term. Okay, he said that there were going to be charge run together that was pending that I've never been back to court on, that he told me that was going to be ran together. There was a great deal of confusion the day of court, because the District Attorney couldn't find the paper work, and he said—the judge asked them could they bring me back a week later; I never went back to court. On May 3rd--- me writing to Georgia Indigency Program, they contacted Mr. Red, and on May 3rd he had Those charges dismissed that was part of my revocation Hearing. Not only that is another charge on my revocation hearing that I'm not guilty of. I'm not guilty of interference with government property, which was dismissed on May 3rd. Is that not right, Mr. Red? I ask for a new revocation hearing.

The Court: Well, let's hear from the lawyer.

Mr. Red, being first duly sworn, testified as follows

Direct Examination by Mr. Blue

Q. Sir, for the record, would you sate your name?

A. Mr. Red

Q. How are you associated with the Petitioner in this case?

A, I believe I was appointed by XXXX County Circuit Defenders to represent him on a probation revocation and on the New charge.

Q. How did you representation develop?

A. Well, the first time—XXXX County doesn't publish revocation hearing calendar notices like they do for trial notices. And, you know, obviously the first time it was on for a revocation calendar, I didn't have a court notice or I would have been there. You know, the people in XXXX County know me; know I'm in the courthouse almost daily for five or six hours a day, so the second time his revocation came up, I'm sure that I was contacted to come, or I just went ahead and, you know, appeared at his hearing.

The Petitioner: Can I say something ,please?

The Court: Not right now. You will get to talk to Him; you can ask any questions in a few minutes, Go Ahead.

Q. Do you recall the underlying charges in XXXX County Being dismissed through your efforts in this case?

Well, the underlying charges, they dismissed that warrant Eventually, on May 3, XXXX; that was done by the District Attorney that was assigned to handle that case- on or about that date.

Q. Do you recall the underlying charges in XXXX County being dismissed through your efforts in this case?

A. Well, the underlying charges, they dismissed the warrant Eventually. On May 3, XXXX, that was done by the District attorney that was assigned to handle that case- on or about that date.

Q. What offense was alleged in this particular warrant that you're referring to?

A. Underage possession of alcohol and obstruction, and the offense of interference with government property.

Q. Was that in XXXX County?

A. That was in XXXX County.

Q. Very generally, could you describe your qualifications?

= CHAPTER 4 =

Are you currently a member in good standing of the State Bar of Georgia?

A. Yes, I've been a member of the State Bar of Georgia since 1984. Since approximately 1997, I deal exclusively in criminal law; I've handled everything from traffic to murder cases. I'm on XXXX County appointed list and am qualified to handle murder cases. And just this past year I handles my first death penalty case as co-counsel.

Q. Were there any issues of the Petitioner's ability to communicate with you effectively during the course of your representation?

A. I don't recall any issues. First of all, you know, there would be notations in the file, because the probation revocation will be, obviously, based upon his prior, either, a plea of guilty or conviction in the case. There was nothing noted in the file that he suffers from any emotional deficiencies I didn't notice any in the file It seemed to be a plea was freely and voluntarily entered with counsel prior to my involvement in the case. What I do recall, when it came on revocation hearing calendar, I believe, and I'm going by memory, that there was a tolling order placed upon Mr. Russell. And it is common, when we go into revocations, we will negotiate with both the District Attorney and the probation officer involved in the case.

Q. what is the effect of tolling order that you mentioned?

A. A tolling order, obviously, would toll his probation time from running during the time that he is absconded from the state; or if he did not leave the State, they couldn't find him.

Q. Do you recall your efforts in resolving the probation revocation?

A. I can tell you, first of all- normally, what I advise the probationer is, that in XXXX County, basically, you can admit the violation and reach an agreement, which you could call a consent revocation. You can admit the violation and be heard before the Court on disposition only, and then the Judge would pass a particular sentence; or you could have a contested revocation hearing. And that's probably the first thing that I said to him when I walked in, you know, to the holding cell to talk to him.

Q. Did you make any promises or guarantees to the Petitioner With respect to any sentence he would receive?

A. No, I can never make any promises or guarantees. I can Tell him what offers are made, and tell him what I believe, to The best of my knowledge, may happen with him. And I do believe That there were negotiations in regard to a detention center Sentence, but based upon the fact that there was a detention center offer of two years or 24 months, he would serve day to day on that. And that's why I believe, in looking back at the consent order that was signed, we reached a three year agreement, because he would be eligible for parole during any time of that three years. It would be my experience on a non violent trial, he would have got out—a non violent crime, that he would have got out of prison much earlier than the complete 24 months he would have served at the detention center.

Q. Did you communicate your opinion in that regard to your Client?

A. I'm sure that I did; I mean, because the consent order speaks to ourselves—speaks to itself. And I always go back and go over that particular consent order with the probationer, because it is essential that everybody signs off- I sign off- the defendant signs off, the District Attorney signs off...

Q. You have referred to consent Revocation Order. Let me show you what has been marked as Respondent's Exhibit Number 8 in this case and ask you to identify it.

A. It is a two page document signed by Judge Yellow, signed by myself, signed by the defendant, and the District Attorney.

Q. Is this the Revocation Order that you were referring to?

A Yes sir.

Q. And also in this packet of Respondents Exhibits, 1 through 8, there appears the underlying Indictment, Plea Questionnaire, Nolle Prosequi, Sentence, Motion to Modify Sentence, Petition for Modification, and Amended Petition for Modification, is correct?

A. Yes

Mr. Blue: Your Honor, we would offer these into the record at this time. We have additional medical Exhibits subsequently, but we would offer these copies that have been provided to the Petitioner.

The Petitioner: Can I say something, Your Honor?

The Court: Sure.

The Petitioner: On this three year, I think, revocation—do you remember, Mr. Red, you said the charges that were pending were going to run together with it, or something? I cant remember exactly all what was said, but it was supposed to have been a two year revocation. And if you see my signature, Your Honor, you can tell that I was totally not competent at the time. And my signature was totally whacked- excuse my language, sir- and it was supposed to be a two year revocation instead of a three year revocation. He stated that he spoke with me about the two year revocation, but the charges that were pending, I never went back to court on those charges; I'm not guilty of them charges. And also – and I cant make parole. All of them charges – I couldn't even read at the time because I had blurred vision fron side effects. I would like to put into evidence at this time my mental health record- the order from XXXX County that – Mr. Green, can I get those records to submit as evidence? The order from the psychiatrist, the medications that I was on at the time. I was never granted a competency hearing, never asked any questions from the Judge, or anything, and I was having severe problems at that time. And just two days prior that my dosage was changed, if you look at the record.

The Court: He's going to testify in a minute, I think. They're going to call him as a witness in just a minute. Are there any questions you want to ask this lawyer?

CROSS EXAMINATION BY PETITIONER RUSSELL

Q. Well, the question is – the deal was, I was going to get credit for time served, it was eight months prior to going to court that I spent incarcerated before. Do you remember that agreement?

A. No, I don't remember that agreement, because I know that when we sign consent orders we sign exactly what was agreed upon and we're very careful to pay credit for time served in every consent order we do in XXXX County, and we run it into the exact date that you get credit for.

Q. Anybody in their right mind who has been locked up eight Months is going to ask for their credit for time served. Did you Request to the Judge for my credit?

A I believe the consent order speaks for itself. And what I remember is probably – I'm pretty sure that you had time in excess of three years that was left on probation, and we reached a deal which would terminated the balance of your sentence.

The Petitioner: I don't remember it that way, Your Honor. I remember that he told me that I was going to get credit for time served; and he spoke of two year detention center time that I was going to do for the revocation, and it would have been a three year deal if they had run those charges...

The Court: I'm going to let you testify in a minute. You can ask him questions right now.

The Petitioner: Okay. I'm through asking him Questions because he's saying he doesn't – that the order Speaks for itself, and I clearly could not even read the Order...

The Court: I'm going to give you a chance to testify in a minute. Is there anything else that you want to ask him?

The Petitioner: No sir.

The Court: Is there anything else that you want to ask him?

= CHAPTER 5 =

RE- DIRECT EXAMINATION BY MR. BLUE

Q. Mr. Red, could you,, for purposes of this record, describe procedurally the process in XXXX County for revocation hearings, such as the one involved in this case?

A Well, currently, they have uncontested admission hearings out at the jail before a Senior Judge, but at the time that Mr. Russell had his probation revocation, he went back to the assigned Judge that had brought a petition against the probationer outlining the allegations in violation of his probation. And you were able to have a contested hearing in which the State would have to either bring in witnesses for your new offense, or certified copies of conviction at that time, or if it was a technical violation, the probation officer would testify to what you did or didn't do. Probation is present there, they have the file, we're able to look at the file to note any tolling orders, to note any calculation of how much time there is left on probation, and what the allegations are. Quit typically, once again, when I get – take a look at a copy of a Petition for revocation, I negotiate with both the probation officer and the D. A. ; I go and tell the client what his rights are in regards to – you know, that he can have a hearing – a contested hearing, or he can make an admission and be heard on the evidence what – you know, on sentencing, and for – you know, he can consent to have an agreement signed. Normally, most Judges don't even bring you before the Court when you sign the consent

Q. Do you recall whether Mr. Russell was brought before the Court in this case?

A. In this case I can't remember whether the Judge would have brought him before the Court at this time. Normally, from memory, the Judge doesn't – he does not, no.

Q. And if the Trial Court does not hold a hearing – a Formal hearing, as you believe was the case here, would there be a transcript available?

A. No, there wouldn't be a transcript.

Q. Is there anything else about this underlying process That you recall?

A. The main thing that I had – I know Mr. Russell had a pending charge against him that – you know, we kind of had a deal with the District Attorney that his new charge if, and when, indicted would run concurrent with his sentence, but, basically, the District Attorney never actually served a warrant on him originally, and they ultimately dismissed the charges. So it was a pending charge for about a year and then they dismissed it, as sometimes goes with XXXX County. This was dismissed on May 3rd. XXXX. I normally take the position, if my client has an active case outstanding, I kind of let a sleeping dog lie and I don't push the District Attorney to indict the case or to formally accuse it. And it just happens that the case was ultimately dismissed, which worked out in favor of my client.

Mr. Blue: Judge, we would also like to get copies made and have a copy of the dismissal of warrant placed In this record, if that is acceptable to the Court.

The Court: All right.

Mr. Blue: There is nothing else I have of this witness with the admission of these various documents that I've identified.

The Court: Do you want to ask him any other questions?

The Petitioner: No sir.

(The witness was excused)

The Court: Call your next witness, please.

Mr. Green, being first duly sworn, testified as follows:

DIRECT EXAMINATION BY MR. BLUE

Q. For the record, would you state your name, please?

A. My name is Mr. Green.

Q. Mr. Green, where are you employed?

A. I'm a mental health counselor at the State Medical Prison.

Q. Are you familiar with the Petitioner, Mr. Jeremiah Russell?

A Yes, I am; he has been at our facility since December on my caseload.

Q. Does he have a certain medical condition that requires Him to be confined at the State Medical Prison?

A. He doesn't have a medical condition, he has a Psychiatric condition that has placed him in our Level Mental Health Supportive Living Unit. Some inmates are considered Impaired to interact with the general population inmates. they are kept out away from the general population inmates. they have special programs in the unit; they go to school with other mental health inmates; they don't interact with the general population inmates very much.

Q Does Mr. Russell have a medical diagnosis that you are familiar with?

A. As far as I know, he has no medical diagnosis now. When he was In XXXX County his medical records talk about a rash.

The Court: About what?

A. A rash. A rash on his face and neck.

Q. Describe for the record, please, your qualifications.

A. I have a Master's Degree in psychology, I work in the the Department of Psychiatry at the Medical College of Georgia for three years; I work for Department of Juvenile Justice for a year before I transferred to the Department of Corrections, where I've been for two years now.

Q. For what period of time have you followed Mr. Russell through your care?

A. He has been on my caseload since December of XXXX.

Q. And I believe you mentioned that you have received his medical records prior to that, is that correct?

A. Right. I did not know him at the time of his revocation, but we did ask for, and received, psychiatric records and medical records from the XXXX County detention facility, and I have reviewed those.

Q. And you have been subpoenaed to this proceeding by the Petitioner, is that correct?

A. That is correct.

Q. Have you had an opportunity to review the Petitioner's Application wherein he alleges certain mental deficiencies?

A. From what I understand, Mr. Russell claims that he was not in the Proper frame of mind to be able to answer to a guilty plea and waive His revocation hearing.

Q. And that would have been as of October the 12th of the year XXXX, Is that correct?

A. Yes sir.

Q. And in connection with those claims, have you reviewed the Nurses Notes and the other medical evidence of record that you access to?

A. I have.

Q. Have you formed any opinions about….

The Petitioner: I object, Your Honor, his opinion is not valid since he's not a psychiatrist, and I don't believe his opinion should be Appropriate for the Court, Your Honor.

The Court: I overrule the objection. Go ahead.

Q. Have you formed any opinions with respect to Mr. Russell Mental condition as od October 12, XXXX?

A Like I said, I did not know Mr. Russell at the time, but if I Can just read the psychiatrist's note from October the 10th two Days before his hearing. This is what the Psychiatrist at the XXXX County Jail said. He said, "Inmate is a little rigid with cogwheeling in both arms. Thinking is clear with no clear with no current complaints. He is now asking to come off razor restriction. No indication of self-abusive Behavior in the past two months. . Frustrated with an attorney who will Not return his calls or letters. Inmate has not to indulge in any self-mutilating Behaviors. The doctor reduced his meds on that date from 20 milligrams to 10, because evidently, he was doing pretty well.

Q. Under what circumstances would it be appropriate to reduce a patient's Dosage?

A Evidently, Mr. Russell had been asking that his medication to be stopped; He was, evidently, not happy with some of the side effects that he was experiencing, like the cogwheeling in his arms. He had some muscle rigidity; he was sleeping a little more than usual; so he was asking for it to be reduced. And the psychiatrist, evidently, thought that he was doing well enough that It could be reduced.

Q. From the medical records available to you, does it appear that Mr. Russell Had any problems communicating with counsel or making a decision on October 12, XXXX?

The Petitioner: I object, Your Honor. How are the records that -- mental health-- I did not get a competency hearing. The records that were taken two days prior To going to court, my medication was decreased. And I remember the day that I was in court I wasn't getting the same medication. And for them to be able to read something two days before that, when my medication was reduced, and to make an opinion, I believe is not right, Your Honor.

= Chapter 6 =

The Court: I overrule the objection. Go head.

Q. What conclusions have you drawn from reviewing the October 10, XXXX Medical entry?

A It appears that, even though Mr. Russell was having some trouble and required the use of an medication agent, he was—and he did experience some side effects from that medication, the psychiatrist clearly says, that thinking is clear with no complaints.

Q. When is the next entry following October 10th that is reflected in the Medical record in the case?

A. October 18th.

Q. Could you describe those records?

A. the psychiatrist said, "Stated I got three years in prison". Asked again to change meds. When told that meds may not be necessary, he asked if he could come off meds. He is doing well with reduced meds and denies any troubles. Mood is upbeat and affect has wide range. " There is no indication that he stopped his medication on that date, there were stopped at a later date.

Q. How long, generally, does it take for a drug, such as the one he was taking that is being weaned from one's dosage, to manifest itself? How long does it take to work its way out of the human bloodstream?

A. First of all, I have to say that I'm not a medical doctor.

Q. Sure.

A. But, generally, we see a change in symptoms' within a couple of days with inmates at prison. When they start an agent or stop it, you usually see full effects within a couple of days; you will see some effects within a day.

Q. But general entries for October the 10th the 18th of XXXX indicate that Mr. Russell was thinking clearly and that he was not having troubles, is that correct?

A. Right.

Mr. Blue: By the way of additional exhibits, we have copies of the Nurses Notes indentified as Exhibit 10, and the psychiatric summary prepared by Mr. Green, Exhibit 11, which we will offer into this record.

The Court: All right.

Mr. Blue: With that, we don't have any further questions.

The Court: Do you want to ask him any question?

CROSS EXAMINATION BY THE PETITIONER:

Q. The question that I would have to ask is – you made an opinion that two days prior to me going to court that they decreased my medication for reasons, right?

A. that is correct.

Q. And can your symptoms vary from day to day?

A. I suppose it's possible, but there is no indication that yours did.

Q. From two days prior- I didn't get seen until eight weeks later. I remember that was in the – that came into the thing and I told him I was doing worse, and he told me not to say nothing about it, and all of this.

Petitioner: I don't have any more questions for him, Your Honor.

The Court: How do you know if a person is actually having troubles or not?

A. That's a tough question. You know, usually—there are times when you can tell, if an inmate is talking to himself or talking to someone who is not there, or acting very paranoid; you know, they may see things that aren't there and try to swat at them, or try to talk to them. If that's not the case—that's what we would consider floridly psychotic, you know, everyone can look at them and tell they are psychotic. The Court: You don't know if they're faking or not though, do you?

A. That's true, they could be faking. You know, for inmates that aren't floridly psychotic, its up to a good interaction between me, or the psychiatrist, and the inmate to talk to them and figure out is this person telling the truth when we ask them if they're hearing voices. Some inmates want drugs for different reasons; some times, you know, have a history of drug abuse and like having medication. Some inmates don't want any medication and will lie to us about hearing the voices until the medication stops and they get worse.

CROSS EXAMINATION BY THE PETITIONER continued:

Q. Can you tell the Court the reason I got sent to the State Medical Prison, that I was taking my medication and that I was trying to hurt myself?

A. Mr. Russell was sent to the State Medical Prison because his mental health level was increased from Level 3 to Level 4. Level 3 inmates have a little bit more responsibility; they have two-man cells. Level 4 inmates, he lives in a single man cell...

Q. The that I asked...

A. His mental health level increased, and that's why he was sent to our facility. He had a history of trying to hurt himself, and refusing medication.

RE-DIRECT EXAMINATION BY MR. BLUE

Q. Do the medical records that you're discussed in this case support an Allegation that are claimed?

A I think that he does have a history of some auditory hallucinations.

Q. How does auditory hallucinations affect one's ability to reason?

A. Most of the people I've worked with, you know, unless they are floridly Psychotic- like we said, unless they're not able to respond to reality and they're only in touch with their psychotic processes, most people can function fairly well, especially when they're on medication, even though they may hear some voices. I have probably ten inmates on my caseload that with high does of medication they still experience voices and they just live with them, they don't like them, but they can handle it. Mr. Blue: That's all I have of this witness, Judge.

The Court: All right. Do you want to ask him anything else?

The Petitioner: No sir.

(The witness was excused)

JEREMIAH RUSSELL, being first duly sworn, testified as follows:

The Court: All right, now you're under oath and you can testify to whatever you want to testify to.

A. Your Honor, they reduced my medication two days prior to going to court, I remember vividly, when I was in the courtroom that I was having some problems. My complaint is, I would like a new revocation hearing because there are charges on the revocation, that I'm not guilty of, making me not be able to get parole. The charges—there were several charges that were dismissed, and there were some charges on there that I wasn't guilty of. And I ask to withdraw my guilty plea to have a new revocation hearing. Not that I'm not guilty of some of the things on the revocation, as far as absconding and not paying my probation- I would like you to have mercy upon me to have a new revocation hearing, Your Honor. I was at the time—I never got a competency hearing from anybody, the Judge, or anything, and I was on heavy medications. I never got a competency hearing to prove was I able at the time to make a right decision. And having misleading statements from counsel wasn't helping the situation any.

The Court: Do you want to ask him any questions?

CROSS EXAMINATION BY MR. BLUE

Q. Mr. Russell, have you had a hearing with the Parole Board?

A. Yes; they said because of the circumstances of my charge that they were denying me parole. And I'm in prison for receiving stolen property probation revocation from XXXX.

Q. Do you know your anticipated parole eligibility release date?

A. It's about three years.

Q. When your probation revocation was held, do you understand that you had more than three years that could have been revoked at that time?

A. Yes; I know that I had seven years probation. And I know if I could get a new revocation hearing that they could take more from me, but the fact is, I had those charges on that revocation that I'm not guilty of. And that's not fair for them—for the Parole Board to not give me parole because there are false allegations on my revocation.

Q. What crimes did you commit before you were revoked?

A. Resisting arrest with violence, possession of powder cocaine, and possession of marijuana.

Q. And how were those charges resolved? Those were in Florida?

A. Those were in Florida. They gave me seven months, and let me go. The police slammed my head on the ground and gave me ten stitches over my eye.

Q. When you went to court on those charges and they were resolved, Did you go to trial or did you enter some type of guilty plea?

A. They gave me time served- seven months time served; a guilty plea.

Q. Okay, you entered a plea of guilty?

A. At the time I had a psychiatrist and a psychologist examine me.

Q. What were the results of those examinations?

A. I don't know the results. I know that they gave me seven months, and I didn't get extradited back because of police brutality.

Mr. Blue: That's all I have, Judge.

The Court: All right.

The Petitioner: I ask the Court, Your Honor, to let me withdraw my guilty plea where I can have a new revocation hearing to have all of this stuff that is inaccurate on my file- on my record cleared up.

The Court: What is inaccurate?

The Petitioner: Okay there are several different charges on here – these charges were dismissed on May 3rd of this year; I'm not guilty of those charges.

The Court: Have you got a history of drug abuse?

The Petitioner: Yes sir.

The Court: All right. Is there anything else that you want to say?

The Petitioner: I just ask Your Honor to have mercy upon my case and grant me to withdraw my guilty plea.

The Court: Is there anything that you want to say, Mr. Blue?

Mr. Blue: Judge, in addition to the procedural obstacles the Petitioner faces, he has not proceeded with and remedies with respect to his probation revocation. And we also contend that this proceeding is brought because his dissatisfaction with the parole process, as a result this would not be the proper form. In addition, though, on the merits, we think his claims are not meritorious. The evidence is undisputed that he – the medical records do not support a claim of mental incompetency at the time the XXXX probation revocation hearing occurred, and that his counsel—his lawyer did not promise him anything, and, in fact, negotiated a successful—pretty favorable and successful plea bargain with respect to the revocation. As a strategical matter, we don't think that that conduct falls within the ambit of Strickland versus Washington. So for all of those reasons we urge the Court to deny the petition.

The Court: I'm going to deny the petition.

(Hearing concluded)

My point for this hearing was that I didn't get eight months credit for time served, I spent three years and eight months for riding that motor cycle. My public defender said I would get the jail time credit, and I was so drugged that I couldn't even see the paper I was signing, I just took his word. Also I couldn't make parole because my paper work was all messed up.

I know I didn't win my hearing, and there were more to the story then what the judge heard, I was on meds at the hearing, and I'm know lawyer. I know crime don't pay and my life has forever changed. I walk a fine line now. Back in those days I was out of control I guess, I wouldn't lesson to anyone and had to learn things the hard way.

I was given a steep sentence and for a long time I felt like I was given injustice, but now I just know it was a tough lesson I learned. What I plan to sure with you next is the second time I went to prison, this time things where so crazy that I really see it as the wildest thing that ever happen. If you read my first book "Insanity" it talks about things that lead to this case I'm going to sure with you. This is the sentencing hearing for Threaten the President. I really didn't mean a threat to the President, but this hearing say things that sure make it look as though I did.

The reader can see how I was given a tuff sentence as the whole case was crazy. I have healed from a lot of tuff challenges. And these court cases give you a chance to see how I was dealt with. When you go to court it can be very nerves some times. In this case I'm about to sure with you, I thought I was going home that day, because my lawyer said I was, and when the DA said all that was said after words I was in chock. I didn't say what I should have said, I couldn't say much at all because the story was much more then the court was aware of. If you read my last book "Insanity" you see how I landed in court this time, for threaten the President.

As you read this remember I really didn't mean a real threat on the President I was trying to get help. After this I will write a letter of apology to the President, he may not be in office any more but I don't just want to reader to know I didn't mean the threat, but want Mr. George W Bush as well. I have been mental challenged going through lock ups because it was never tough on me.

Here is the transcript where I was sentenced to prison for a crime of being mental challenged, I was more then challenged but under what I believe was MK-Ultra of some sort. If you don't know what that means just Google MK-Ultra.

Never again will I go to prison or a hospital. I learned the years I was living on the streets that the only way to get into a hospital was threaten your life or someone else's. There was times I went into the hospital just to take a brake from the many troubles I had. I learned that someone like myself in the court of law can be made out as someone their not, as you will see in this transcript your about to read.

Chapter 7

UNITED STATES DISTRICT COURT

FOR THE NORTHERN DISTRICT OF XXXX

UNITED STATES OF AMERICA,

-VS

CASE# XXXXXX

JEREMIAH GENE RUSSELL,

DEFENDANT.

TRANSCRIPT OF SENTENCING PROCEEDINGS

BEFORE THE HONORABLE JUDGE

UNITED STATES DISTRICT COURT

THURSDAY, MAY 29

APPEARANCES:

ON BEHALF OF THE GOVERNMENT:

MS. ONE

ASSISTANT UNITED STATES ATTORNEY

ON BEHALF OF THE DEFENDANT: MR. TWO

(Thursday, May 29, 2008; Atlanta, Georgia.)

THE COURT: Good Morning

MS ONE: Good Morning, Your Honor.

MR TWO: Good Morning.

THE COURT: Good Morning, Mr. Russell.

THE DEFENDANT: Good Morning, Sir.

THE COURT: The Court will adopt the findings of fact and the conclusions of law in the presentence report to which neither side has registered an objection.

There are three objections by the defendant. We begin with the base offense level is 12 for this offense, making a threat against the President of the United States.

And then in paragraph 14, we have a dispute. The probation report - - presentence report says that the offense should be increased 2 levels because the offense involved more than two threats. The defendant has objected to this finding asserting that there was only one threat, and I'll hear from both sides on that. It seems to me like it's one threat, but I want to hear from the Government. Sounds to me like he was kind of repeating what he said before. And it was during the interview and it's - - I'll just tell you my inclination at this point is not to reduce and give a 4-level reduction. I don't think that's warranted. But on the other hand, it seems to me like, viewed properly, it's one threat.

What do you think, Ms. One?

MS. ONE: Well, Your Honor, I believe that the guidelines provide for this to be considered more than two threats. Although it was to the same victim, the guidelines do say that it can be to the same victim as long as there are more than two threats. And here, while I agree with you it was all a threat to the same person, that it, the President of the United States, it was given at least three different times. First was over the 911 call where he went on for quite some time about killing the President. Secondly was to Corporal - - I believe his name was Peavy, Corporal Peavy.

THE COURT: Right.

MS. ONE: Who responded to the scene. He reiterated the threat to Corporal, and then again to Special Agent who I have here in the courtroom if the Court would like to hear from him, although there's no dispute about the facts. But to Special Agent the defendant repeated the threat again and actually went into a little bit more detail, because Special Agent asked the defendant as noted here in the presentence report why he wanted to kill the President. And it again, talking about Iraq and talking about God and why he wanted to do it. He even mentioned the United Nations maybe out to kill the President, and so if someone told him to kill him, he'd kill him.

The - - so while it was the same threat in the sense that it was all to President Bush, he reiterated the threat over and over and over again. And I think the spirit of this guideline, Your Honor, is that they would receive a reduction or at least not get an enhancement if it was simply one threat because there's some accounting form someone making an off-the-cuff comment or a serious threat to the President but only making it once and then reconsidering and understanding the consequences of their actions. This defendant just simply continued to make the threat. And, of course, that is why the defendant is here in court today.

If the defendant had merely made one threat, the Secret Service has a lot of discretion, along with the U. S. Attorney's Office, about whether to bring cases, and sometimes people will write a letter. Secret Service has to go and visit every single person that makes a threat to the President. What this defendant did, of course, drew the attention of the entire federal government because of what he did. This was more than someone making an off –the-cuff threat as - -

THE COURT: Well, would you not agree that for the specific offense characteristic that would result in a 2-level enhancement to apply, there must be more than two threats?

MS. ONE: That's correct, I agree.

THE COURT: Which of course is three.

MS. ONE: There are three.

THE COURT: Okay. One is the 911 operator. Two is when he's being interviewed by Special Agent. And where's the third one?

MS. ONE: Well, two, is actually to Corporal.

THE COURT: - - and talks to him right then and there?

MS. ONE: Well, there's actually - - and this is why I have Special Agent here, Your Honor. While the presentence report talks about Corporal coming, the presentence report doesn't go into full detail about what occurred when Corporal was there. Special Agent has reviewed the transcript - - or the videotaped interview with the defendant - - or, I'm sorry, was it audio taped? The patrol car video of Corporal talking to the defendant where the threats are reiterated. So that's why I made sure the Special Agent is here so he could tell the Court, if the Court wishes to hear from him - -

THE COURT: Yeah, I want to hear from him. I want to hear what exactly happened.

MS. ONE: Yes, sir. Then we'll call Special Agent

MR. TWO: Judge, before this happened, I've never been provided a copy of the videoape that he's going to be testifying to. And I would think that rather than have him summarize what he thinks is on the videotape based on his recollection, the best evidence is the actual videotape itself. And I think that we need to see the videotape rather than - - in order to really get a flavor for what it's about. I mean, as to his interview with Mr. Russell, I have no problem with him testifying about that.

THE COURT: Uh-huh. Ms. One?

MS. ONE: Hearsay is admissible in sentencing, Your Honor.

MR. TWO: It may be admissible, Judge, but I think some semblance of notice of the existence of a statement of the defendant would be required to be turned over prior to sentencing.

MS. ONE: That was turned over to the defense, Your Honor, at the beginning of this case. Ms. Three was well aware that there was patrol car video of this incident.

MR. TWO: Well, we don't have the patrol car video and that was not provided to us.

THE COURT: I'm going to overrule the objection. I'll hear the testimony.

SPECIAL AGENT, having been duly sworn, was examined and testified as follows:

THE COURTROOM DEPUTY CLERK: Will you state your name and spell it for the record, please?

THE WITNESS: Special Agent

DIRECT EXAMINATION

BY MS. ONE:

Q. And, Special Agent, you're an agent with the Secret Service; is that right?

A. That is correct.

Q. How long have you been a Secret Service agent?

A. Since 2003.

Q. And as part of your responsibilities, do you investigate threats against the President and other officials of the Government?

A. It is.

Q. Were you assigned to investigate this threat against the President that involved Mr. Jeremiah Gene Russell?

A. Yes, I was.

Q. Would you describe for the Court, please, how you became involved in this investigation?

33

A. I received a telephone call in our field office from the street - - actual interview of Corporal from the patrol car stated that he had just come upon the scene and wanted some guidance on what to do. At that time I asked what was going on, and he said he had made a threat to 911. He didn't have the exact threat at that time.

He stated that the defendant had reiterated a threat to him, saying that he was on his way to kill the President, he had walked from Alabama to do so. This interview actually took place in Cherokee County on I-75, so it was quite a distance that he had walked.

At that time I asked what the status was, and he said he was not under arrest. He was at that time just detained for investigative detention.

I said if - - if the defendant - - or - - at the time, if the individual was willing to go with him to the patrol house, the precinct. He did voluntarily go there. He was not under arrest at that time. I responded at that time to the - - to the precinct and conducted a interview at that time.

Q. Have you had the opportunity to speak with Corporal since your phone conversation with him when he was talking with Jeremiah Gene Russell back in November of XXXX?

A. that is correct.

Q. Have you also had the opportunity to review the patrol car video of Corporal's discussion with Mr. Russell?

A. I have.

Q. Would you describe - - have you also listened to the 911 call made by Mr. Russell?

A. Yes. I have that tape, also.

Q. Would you describe the different threats and all the things that Mr. Russell said on the 911 call to Corporal and also during your interview regarding the President?

A. Okay. First, the 911 call was a pay phone call from a small gas station in Cherokee County. The 911 dispatcher asked first what the nature of the call was. The defendant stated his name and said he was going to – thinking about killing the President. The 911 operator then had a slight pause in there, turned around and asked another question of: What was that? And she [sic] said: I'm on my way to kill the President. Turned around, dispatched a vehicle, Sheriff's Office. It was Corporal that responded. At that time he - -

THE COURT: But he also told the 911 operator something to the effect of "Come get me"?

= CHAPTER 8 =

THE WITNESS: Correct. She did ask exactly where he was. He said: I'm where this phone is. You can come get me.

At that time the patrol car arrived. The video was not turned on at the beginning. The corporal exited the vehicle, began to conduct a street interview at that time, found that there was a probable reason to turn on the video, so he turned on the vehicle audio and video at that time.

The - - the defendant went ahead and restated that he was on his way to kill the President. He said he had been chased by dogs all the way from Alabama. There was multiple statements in there to the turn, and then the phone call was made to us for guidance on where to go with this style of case.

THE COURT: And then you interviewed him?

THE WITNESS: I did. I responded to the precinct in Cherokee County and conducted an interview with another agent of ours.

Q. (By Ms. ONE): And what did - -

THE COURT: How long did your interview last?

THE WITNESS: Interview lasted approximately an hour.

THE COURT: All right. What happened?

THE WITNESS: During the interview, it was reiterated that he understood that it was a crime to threaten the President. He was not afraid to go to jail for that - - or go to prison I believe was the term. I was leaning towards some sort of mental defect at the time or some sort of lack of medication.

We asked the defendant if he'd be willing to go for a psychiatric evaluation, which he was, and he signed himself in at the regional hospital for a in-house psychiatric evaluation.

Q. (BY MS. ONE): What other sort of things did he talk to you about the President and why he wanted to kill the President?

A. He claimed that the President had an order out to kill him and that he was going to kill the President in order to circumvent that order. He had also made comments about the President was killing children in Iraq and that he had written a book, "J Mack's Journey Through Hell," that kept coming up and had statements to the same in it.

Q. Did he talk about the United Nations?

A. He did. He mentioned the United Nations. There was multiple comments that were made of a delusional aspect that made no real sense in the threat itself.

Q. Did he talk about - - what did he say specifically about the United Nations and the President?

A. I - - without reviewing the video right here at this time, I can't say exactly.

Q. But you recall him talking about the United Nations and the President?

A. He did, yes. He made statements to that - - to that nature. I don't know the exact content of them without that transcript.

Q. And you said your interview with the defendant lasted about an hour?

A. Correct.

Q. Did he say anything else to you about the President other than what you've described?

A. Again, without having - - without having that - - it was to that general nature.

Q. Did he talk a little bit about God or the Holy Spirit?

A. He did. There was many mentions of religion throughout this. Again, made no - - at the time it was delusional and there was no real semblance to it.

MS. ONE: Thank you. That's all the questions I have.

THE COURT: All right. Any Cross?

MR. TWO: Judge, again, now that he has testified and that he's stated that he's relied on this videotape, I would ask that - - pursuant to Rule 26. 2 that the videotape be disclosed to me so I could adequately question him at this point. I have no idea what's on there and can't question him about it.

THE COURT: All right. I'm going to overrule your request.

MR. TWO: Okay

THE COURT: Because I understand you've had the opportunity or his counsel has had the opportunity or his counsel has had the opportunity to review the tape already.

MR. TWO: As I understand, that's just not true. I - - it apparently there may be some word that there was a tape out there, but that tape has never been provided to us. It's not in our files, and it's not even listed in the presentence report. So, we're - - I'm standing here completely blind-sided by this.

THE COURT: Well, there's nothing - - I'll be honest with you. There's nothing that he said today that really impacts my decision in this. And to be candid with you, I'm inclined to not enhance by 2 points.

MR. TWO: Okay,

THE COURT: - - that his testimony regarding what Officer, - - or Corporal did during his interview with the defendant that was captured on the - - that was captured on the tape is not going to affect how I sentence him today.

MR. TWO: Okay. Well, let me just ask a few questions.

THE COURT: You may if you want, but I've already - -

MR. TWO: I do. I feel like I need to make a couple of points for the record just so I'm clear.

MR. TWO: I do. I feel like I need to make a couple of points for the record just so I'm clear.

THE COURT: That's fine. Okay.

CROSS EXAMINATION

BY MR. TWO

Q. Good morning, Agent.

A. Good morning.

Q. Now, when - - as I understand it from your testimony, that Officer when he arrived at the Amoco station did not know exactly what the statements were that Mr. Russell made to the 911 operator; is that correct?

A. He received a dispatch from the 911 operator to a disturbance call for a 911 - - not a hang up, but a 911 call. He responded and then began his street interview at that time.

Q. And as part of his street interview, he asked Mr. Russell, "What did you tell the 911 operator?" Right?

A. Yes, sir.

Q. Okay. And Mr. Russell then responded, "I told the 911 operator I was going to kill the President"?

A. That is correct.

Q. Okay. And Similarly, when you took him in - - well, when you went to interview him when he was at the County Sheriff's Office, you asked him, "What did you say to the 911 operator?" Correct?

A. That was one of my questions, yes.

Q. And he said, "I told the 911 operator that I was going to kill the President"?

A. That is correct. It was reiterated, yes.

Q. Okay. And, so, when you say reiterated, it's reiterated in response to your question?

A. He did answer all of my questions, correct.

Q. And you actually did an affidavit in support of the criminal complaint, did you not?

A. Yes, I did.

Q. And in that criminal complaint, you indicated that you asked the subject aout the call he made to the 911 in his statements to Corporal and he responded, "I'm going to kill the President"?

A. That is correct.

Q. Okay.

MR. TWO: Thank you, Judge. I have no further questions –

Q. (BY MR. TWO): Oh, and you mentioned also that during your interview, he was delusional?

A. Correct.

Q. And you were, you said, leery about his mental condition?

A. Correct.

Q. And felt the need to basically immediately check him into Peachford?

A. He was not directly checked into Peachford. He was asked if he would sign himself in for and evaluation, which he did.

Q. And you thought that was necessary?

A. Correct.

Q. Appropriate?

A. I did.

MR. TWO: Thank you.

THE COURT: All right. You may step down. Thank you, sir.

All right. The Court is going to sustain the defendant's objection to the enhancement by 2 levels based on the specific offense characteristic that the offense involved more than two threats. I don't think that it did involve more than two threats. I think it involved a threat that was made to the 911 operator and then the threat was restated to Officer – to Corporal with the Sheriff's Department and then again to Special Agent. I think that it just depends on how you defind a new threat each time. But I think in fairness, this should not be regarded as three threats to the President's life. That's – that's not my take on it at all. And, so, I'm going to uphold the defendant's objection.

And, so, we now have again a base offense level of 12. And then having sustained that objection, the next objection is whether or not 3 more levels should be added because the intended victim, President George W. Bush, is a government officer and the offense of conviction was motivated by such status. Mr. Two, I'll hear from you on this one.

MR. TWO: Okay. Judge, actually, I'm happy to go to that one as well. I still think there's the separate issue within the guideline before we get to the Chapter 3 enhancements.

THE COURT: Right.

MR. TWO: I stil think there's an objection relating to the 4-level reduction.

THE COURT: It was kind of a double – a double objection, so I'll hear from you on whether or not there should be a 4-level reduction based on Section 2A6. (b) (5) –

MR. TWO: Right.

THE COURT: -- of the guidelines.

MR. TWO: Right. And first of all, let me start with the easy part. Paragraph 11 of the presentence report makes a finding to which there's no objection and I presume has been adopted by this Court –

41

THE COURT: It has.

MR. TWO: -- that says that thre appears to be very little likelihood that defendant would carry out the threat. That I think is important –

THE COURT: Why?

MR. TWO: Well, because there's a two-part test here. It says that the offense involved a single incident evidencing little or no deliberation, decrease by 4 levels. Clearly, he's not -- I think – and the part he's not intending to carry out the threat goes to the little deliberation part of it.

The other part of it is –

THE COURT: Well, let he ask you: Did he in fact walk from Alabama?

MR. TWO: I believe he walked and hitchhiked and found his way there from Alabama.

THE COURT: Well, you know, it seems to me that there had to be substantial deliberation between Alabama and Georgia.

MR. TWO: Well, there – I don't know how –

THE COURT: Not counting what deliberation he might have engaged in prior to that time.

MR. TWO: Well, there may be some deliberation about walking from Alabama to Georgia, but I don't know that that's necessarily deliberation to kill the President while coming there, because – part of the important part of this and part of the overall picture is he was delusional. He was – I mean, frankly, in my personal view, he was insane. And that plays into it.

THE COURT: I don't know how much the Government agrees or disagrees with that, but the fact that – well, anyway, go ahead.

MR. TWO: Well, let's talk a little bit about the idea of individual threats. I think what we – what we just heard is he made the threat to 911. That's the one threat. I – no dispute about that. After that he gets contacted by – the police come out and investigate him, and they said what did you say and he repeats it. That repeating a threat in response to an interrogation, asking him what you said previously, is not a second or third instance of making a threat.

THE COURT: I think it's not necessarily a separate several instance of a threat, but I think it can be. And I'm not really sure. I kind of gave him the benefit of the doubt.

MR. TWO: I appreciate that.

THE COURT: I can easily imagine a person in his shoes calling 911, making a threat, and then when the investigating officer arrives and then the investigating special agent arrives after that, the accused repeating the threat in such a way as to support a finding that it was a separate threat. I gave him the benefit of the doubt. But I'm not suggesting that it was just so clear that what happened was he made a threat and then he was asked what did you say and he merely repeated what he said. I have the impression from reading the report that there was more to it than that, that he was – he was clinging more to his intention than one might infer if one were to conclude that he were merely repeating what he had one time stated.

MR. TWO: I appreciate the Court's position and understand it. And part of my argument, I think, has – there's a bigger – there's a small picture as we detail guidelines and there's a big picture of what's actually going on. And if I may sort of step back to the big picture of what's actually goin on. And if I may sort of step back to the big picture to give some perspective to the small picture, I think that may .

= CHAPTER 9 =

THE COURT: All right.

MR. TWO: -- help with this argument.

THE COURT: All right.

MR. TWO: Judge, I'd like to tender to the Court Defendant's Exhibits 1 and 2 which I've probided to the Government. The Defendant's Exhibit 1 is a psychiatric evaluation done by a Dr. at Behavioral Health Systems on November 16th , which would have been the day after his arrest.

THE COURT: Right.

MR. TWO: And whre he would have been checked in. And Defendant's Exhibit 2 is the discharge summary for Mr. Russell ten days later on November 26th, 2006. And dthese evaluations detail his mental condition at the time of the events.

THE COURT: Okay. Acute psychosis.

MR. TWO: Acute psychosis. You know, describing him as, you know, having auditory hallucinations, delusional, psychotic, homicidal ideation toward the President. Says you need to read a book about me,. He's described as being very paranoid, grandiose, delusional, having delusional thought content. They say his intelligence and memory cannot be tested at this time due to acute psychosis. It talked about the schizophrenia.

And interestingly enough, have a Global Assessment Functioning score of 10 to 15. The Global Assessment Functioning is basically a scale of how you're doing in life that goes on a scale of 1 to 100 with 100 being no problems at all and, you know, 1 being the lowest possible. He's at 10 to 15 because of this severe mental illness. So he is at pretty much the lowest possible range you can get.

Similarly, in his discharge summary, which describes his behavior on the unit and the observations of him – or it is very consistent with the delusional thinking, but talk about hearing God talking to him, having a special sense of smell, fear of having chemical weapons residue on him. Talking about gases entering his room, walking around the unit with a mask or a towel over his nose because of the gases. I think at one point he's turning his shower on and off to get steam in his room, again concerned about the chemical weapon residue and gas. And basically described as psychotic at the time of discharge ten days later.

And then again, that is consistent with the findings that they made in Springfield in December when he went up there and was found incompetent to stand trial for over a year because of his mental illness, which included statements in which he talked about speaking seven different languages, having shot lightening bolts from his fingertips, communicate with others without them being there. At one point talks about acquiring special powers this past Halloween when he painted his face, climbed a mountain, and the Archangel Michael appeared to him.

Clearly Mr. Russell was delusional at the time he's making any of these statements. And to assess any level of deliberation or real mental processing on them I think is a stretch.

THE COURT: All right. I understand your argument.

All right. Let me hear from the Government in response to that.

MS. ONE: I would also note for the record, Your Honor, that I was given these particular reports this morning don't object to their admission, however.

I would also note for the record that – just because I want the Court to know because I haven't been in front of this Court all that often, as an AUSA, I'm a former ADA. I have an open-file discovery policy. Not everyone in my office does, but I certainly do. I provided a copy of the patrol car camera to Ms. Three specifically, without her requesting it, because we never indicted this case. This case went directly from the defendant off being evaluated under criminal complaint to the defendant pleading to an information.

THE COURT: Right.

MS. ONE: The Government provided everything in its file to Ms. Fleming. Perhaps Mr. Two did not have the opportunity to see that DVD. I don't know. But the Government provided that to Ms. Three, and I wanted the Court to be aware of that.

THE COURT: I understand that.

MS. ONE: Since Mr. Two said that was not true, I want the Court to know that it is in fact true.

THE COURT: Well, he said he didn't have it and –

MS. ONE: That may very well be true.

THE COURT: And I think that's true.

MS. ONE: But Ms. Three did.

THE COURT: But I also think it's true that you gave it to the defendant's counsel.

MS. ONE: Yes, sir.

As far as his argument that this offense – that he merits a 4-level reduction because the offense showed little or no deliberation and simply a single instance of a threat, the Court's aware of the Government's position on whether or not there was a single instance of a threat.

THE COURT: Right.

MS. ONE: And while I understand your reasons for not enhancing him, I do think that the – that decreasing 4 levels doesn't make any sense, because the Court –

THE COURT: I agree. I agree with you.

MS. ONE: -- because the Court – you do have the evidence about him making the threat, reiterating it. What I think is important to the Government in this case – well, lots of important things in this case, but most importantly, as far as this issue in particular, is the detail that the defendant went into --

THE COURT: Yeah. I mean –

MS. ONE: -- about why he wants to. This wasn't just I said I wanted to kill the President and then , yes, I did tell the 911 operator that and, yes, I did tell the patrol officer that. That's not what we have here. If we did, this situation might be a little bit different.

Instead he went into detail, talking about the United Nations and God, talking about the President killing children in Iraq. I mean, he went into his reasons that he wants to kill the President. And has, you know, traveled from Alabama to get over to the President. I don't know what the President's schedule was at that time, but the President certainly visits xxxx on occasion and has done so in the past and probably will do so in the future. And, so, I do not believe that the facts of this case merit a reduction under that particular subsection.

THE COURT: Well, yeah. And the -- it's a legal question of whether or not Section 2A6. 1 (b)(5) applies, specifically whether or not the offense involved a single instance evidencing little or no deliberation. And the Court will overrule the defendant's objection—or objection and request that the 4-level reduction be applied. All right. So, again, we started at 12 and we're still at 12, and now the question is whether 3 levels should be added as a victim related adjustment pursuant to Section 3A1. 2 (a) on the grounds that the intended victim, President George W. Bush, is a government officer and the offense of conviction was motivated by such states. And I'll hear from you, Mr. Two.

MR. TWO: I hate to sound like a bit of a broken record on this, Judge, but—

THE COURT: Oh, I think your argument is that he – goes to the words "motivated".

MR. TWO: Exactly. You know, the – Mr. Russell was delusional and looking for help and trying to get into a – a treatment place and get into a safe place. He claims he's being chased by dogs from Alabama into XXXX and that people are trying to kill him, including the President.

And that what he's doing—and, in fact, he's says, "I'm Jeremiah Russell. I'm right here at Amoco. Come get me. "

THE COURT: right. The problem it that—the problems is that if we view this as a cry for help, which the evidence certainly would allow one to draw the inference, he nevertheless made a threat to the President and he – and his threat was laden with facts that are specific to the President, or t least in his mind were specific to the President, such as killing children in Iraq and, you know, carrying out the orders of God, that type of thing, to carry out his threat. I mean, they'd all involved the President in his capacity as a government officer, and he was motivated by that status.

It—you know, if you try to say he was not motivated by that status, again it's like you acknowledged at the beginning which is that you're just repeating your argument. I don't fault you for that because I understand your theory, and that's precisely what I would probably assert if I were in your shoes. And if we had a case here where it was a cry for help and nothing else, I would agree with you. But it wasn't just a cry for help. It was a bona fide threat to take the life of the President of the United States. And clearly it was because of his—he's a government officer and it was motivated by his status because he is president. I mean, that's why he did it.

Now, he could have chosen to cry for help in some other way. He could have—and I understand your response to that is maybe that, well he couldn't because of his problem. And I understand that. But nevertheless, the law says that if anybody does this, it's a crime. And the law further says that if the – in computing what the sentence should be, if the threat is against a government officer and it was motivated by that status you have to add 3 points. There's no way I cannot add 3 points. My hands are tied.

MR. TWO: well I would add one more level to this is that he did not have the ability to form the requisite intent to threaten the President, and – because of his delusional capacity. And while he has plead guilty to it, that was his choice not to raise an insanity defense, I don't –

THE COURT: Well, even if that's true, the question is: Was he motivated by the President's status as a government officer? And there's no doubt about that that it was.

MR. TWO: Well, but motivation requires intention.

THE COURT: Oh, I don't know—I don't know that motivation necessarily requires intention. It may require understanding. I'm not sure. But, you know the guidelines don't make an exception that you're attempting to propose here. The guidelines—would you acknowledge that?

MR. TWO: I knowledge that the guidelines don't say what—that— that that is—that they don't have an exception for insanity.

THE COURT: The guidelines do not say that if a person is suffering from mental instability, the Court is authorized to find that he—that the defendant therefore lacked the capacity to have a motivation to kill the President based on his status as a government officer. There's just no carved-out exception for that.

MR. TWO: While there is no specifaclly written carved-out expression of that in the guidelines, I think the Court has the inherent authority to find that he lacked the ability to make the necessary—the – make that kind of threat and have that kind of motivation based on his mental capacity.

THE COURT: Well, I'm going to—

MR. TWO: And, so. Again, I understand the Courts's position on it —

THE COURT: Yeah.

MR. TWO: -- and I wanted to make sure the record's clear—

THE COURT: Sure.

MR. TWO: --That, one, the motivation was to get help. Two, the statements were made by a delusional individual. And that, three, I think there's a real Eighth Amendment problem holding and enhancing a person for an offense based on statements made while they are delusional. So, for all three of those reasons, I think that it would be appropriate not to include this enhancement, and part of that certainly is a 3553 argument that is to come in a few minutes.

THE COURT: All right. The Court will respectfully overrule the defendant's objection in regards and will add 3 levels from 12 to 15, and — which is where we are now. And the defendant has accepted responsibility, so how many points will we be reducing here; 2 or 3?

The Probation Officer: Actually, Your Honor, due to the acceptance of responsibility under 3E!. 1 (a), he would only be entitled to 2 levels.

THE COURT: Because--- that's what I thought.

The Probation Officer: The adjusted offense level was reduced down to 15.

THE COURT: Right.

The Probation Officer: And, thus, he's not over the 16 levels that would be necessary for the additional point.

THE COURT: Yes, sir. I agree.

MR. TWO: I do believe that's correct, Judge.

THE COURT: Okay. So what we have is a total offense level of 13. And I'll sustain the defendant's objection regarding paragraph 48 of report. It doesn't affect the guideline computation, and — but I will rule in the defendant's favor on that. And that means that we have an offense level of 13. And the defendant has a Criminal History Category of V, which means that the sentencing range is between 30 and 37 months. The fine guideline range, how would that change for us?

The Probation Officer: Your Honor, the fine guideline range would be 3,000 to 30,000.

THE COURT: Yeah, that's what I thought. Okay. Thank you, sir.

Restitution's not involved. There will be a $100 special assessment. And the supervised release period is between 2 and 3 years. That's the range of punishment.

Do you both agree with that?

MS. ONE: Yes, sir.

MR. TWO: Yes, sir.

THE COURT: Okay. I'll hear from the Government as to what sentence should be.

MS. ONE: First, Your Honor, I would agree with the defense om one thing today, and that is that the defendant was psychotic and paranoid schizophrenic at the time of the crime. I would argue he still is. He's on medication, so I suppose medically he's not defined that way. But the day the defendant stops taking his medication, the defendant again becomes psychotic and paranoid schizophrenic which makes him dangerous. Which is why the Government in this case recommends that the Court sentences the defendant to the maximum under the guidelines which is 37 months.

While this defendant, as the defense argues—and with some justification, I can see their point—the defendant was crying out for help. And that may be true in the sense that he called and said here I am, I'm thinking about killing the President, come and get me. Oh the other hand, there are a couple of things in this case that make this a little bit different from just a defendant who's looking to get out of the rain or looking to get treatment, which I really do not think was his motivation given his conduct during his evaluation periods, which was quite lengthy.

In fact, I think possibly the defendant was looking to get out of the rain, looking for a meal, that may be true, but if he was not motivated about the President and his disagreement with the President's policies or whatever it is he hates about the President, he certainly could have threatened the gas station attendant there at Amoco. The police would have come. He could have said I've got a rifle. I'm going to kill a bunch of people. The police would have come. He could have said I'm about to blow my brains out. I'm at the Amoco. The police would have come. But the defendant elected and plead guilty and waived, by the way, his rights to an insanity hearing, agreeing he was competent, and admitted to threatening the life of the President of the United States and told the Secret Service why. And that's the crux of this and what makes this defendant so dangerous.

Mr. Two is, I'm confident, as he sort of has already, going to argue to the Court that this defendant had no real intention of killing the President. He made the threat, although as Mr. Two has said, he thinks he didn't even know what he was doing. I disagree.

═ Chapter 10 ═

But Mr. Two will certainly argue to the Court that he had no means or intention of carrying it out. I disagree, respectfully. Once the defendant got into custody at Peachford, he attacked his roommate with a towel bar. He ripped it off a wall and attacked him with a towel bar. Mr. two and I talked about this prior to the hearing. He agrees with me on that. That is a fact. The defendant showed he was capable of violence.

The defendant has a lot of reasons for what he says is hatred of the President Bush. Unfortunately for President Bush, it's not uncommon opinion all over the blogs. People believe the President is guilty of war crimes. I read an article just yesterday about someone trying to effect a citizen's arrest in England on Former Ambassador to the UN Bolton for war crimes, they said, that they were trying to arrest because they really believe that the Ambassador and President and his entire staff are guilty of war crimes. And I submit to the Court that this defendant's behavior shows that he is on the same level, on a very important level, believes the same thing.

And while we don't have any evidence in this case of the defendant having a gun or having written out a plan to kill the President or getting the President's schedule, that doesn't mean he couldn't have. And while I certainly admire the Secret Service protection of the President and all the people that they are charged with protecting, as the Court is well aware, they'er not perfect. No system is perfect. And a very determined defendant, just like John Hinkly, can get to the President.

This defendant, when he gets out of prison, is a risk to the President of the United States. George W. Bush will probably still be President when the defendant gets out—well, possibly not. I believe he's been in fro 18 months. Depends on the sentence the Court finds is reasonable in this case. But George W. Bush will certainly be around, God willing, after he leaves office and there will be another president in office that perhaps this defendant will disagree with their policies and decide the time is now to act.

A single man with a weapon, any kind of a weapon, might be able to get to the President, but can certainly get to the Secret Service. He could drive a car through the Secret Service line, he could stab someone, he could hurt anyone around the President protecting the President or the President himself.

And the defendant's very mental condition that Mr. Two uses, and I agree the defendant suffers from, as an excuse here or as somehow meaning the defendant is incapable of the kind of violence or planning necessary to commit an offense against a public official is the very reason I believe he's dangerous and why I think a reasonable sentence in this case is the high end of the guideline range, because he is the text kind of person that gets there. He is John Hinkly. That is who tried to kill President Reagon. He is Sirhan Sirhan. I mean these are the people.

It's not been history—it has not been cabal of people, at least not that's been proven, who has assassinated our presidents. John F. Kennedy was assassinated by one man with one gun; a rifle; an old rifle. President Reagon was shot by one man with one gun. Candidate Kennedy was killed with one man in a convention hall and one gun. Lincoln, one man, one gun. And at least from Kennedy forward, they had Secret Service protection. But they're human, too, and one man with one gun can do it.

And unfortunately guns are easy to get. Mr. Two said—might say, well, he's a convicted felon now, he's certainly not going to be able to get a gun. That's just not the case unfortunately. And this office and all our agents do everything they can to keep illegal guns off the streets, but it's impossible.

This defendant has shown that he wants to kill the President. He said it. He explained it. And he is—he has mental condition that makes him a risk to this President and to any other President, to many public

53

officials. Perhaps he'll turn his attention to the governor or some public official without Secret Service protection who's much easier to kill , who he decides is killing children or doing something that he doesn't like.

Mr. Russell is a dangerous man. And the Government believes as long this Court can keep him in prison, we're recommending the high end of the guideline, is important to do so because the Government submits that this defendant when he gets out of prison may or may not continue to take his medication. He's not being forcibly medicated now, and certainly when he gets out of prison, nobody's going to make him take it. If he doesn't want to take it, we exactly back where we were in Nov of XXXX with the defendant raving about presidential crimes and the President having some order to kill him out and he's got to defend himself. And then we have another very dangerous man, who's probably learned his lesson about calling 911 and making his threat. I'd submit to the Court I find it highly unlikely to think he's going to warn us again.

Jeremiah Russell is a threat to this President and any other, and I'd ask you to keep him in prison for the maximum allowed under the guidelines in this case and that's 37 months.

THE COURT: Thank you, ma'am. Mr. Two?

MR. TWO: Judge, our entire system of justice and our entire country and Government is judged and is rightfully judged on how we treat the weakest among us, how we treat our poor, how we treat our homeless, how we treat or insane. And our—the measure of humanity really depends on it. It's very easy to treat the rich rappers well because they are rich, but how we treat someone like Jeremiah Russell who – at the time of the offense is not all that much different tham somebody that you could walk out this courtroom and see on the street who has no cloths or no – dressed in rags and is talking and ranting to himself. And whether we punish Mr. Russell because he was in that mental condition that he could not help. Whether we sentence him to maximum or whether we sentence to what I'm asking for, which is 18 months, is really what our system is – is all about and what it's going to be judged on.

Mr. Russell in my view was not criminally liable or criminally responsible on the day he made these threats. We see the reports. He was out of his mind.

THE COURT: Now, wait a minute. He plead guilty.

MR. TWO: I don't disagree with that.

THE COURT: Okay. So he's – he is criminally--

MR. TWO: He has accepted responsibility.

THE COURT: Yeah. So he is criminally liable and he is criminally responsible, correct to what you just said'

MR. TWO: Well, he had the opportunity to -- had an agreement with the Government to plead not guilty by reason of insanity and he chose not to do that. He's competent now. He's been medicated for over a year, takes his medication. He is--that was his decision to make. And he agreed to subject himself to a -- to the--to a guilty plea and to the-- what flows from that. And, so, on technical legal level he is--the Court correct, he's criminally responsible. But on a real level, how he was at the time--and he -- I -- you know, there was -- there's not a finding of it, but I think those reports are very clear, he was insane at the time this happened. And, so, in my view --

THE COURT: well, the Government's acknowledged that.

MR. TWO: Right. And we don't punish insane people. We don't -- we don't excute insane people because they don't understand and they're not criminally liable. And that's something that goes back to the 1600s there's documented cases saying that.

And, you know, even in Suprema Court case law, there's a case, I believe, California vs. Brown where the Supreme Court has knowledge that even to – when somebody's not insane, but – that this is quote from Justice O' Connor, which is California vs Brown, 470 US 538, which is 1987. It talks about a long-held belief in this society that defendants who commit criminal acts that are attributable to disadvantaged backgrounds or to mental or emotional problems may be less culpable than a defendant who have no such.

Clearly, Mr. Russell, because of his condition at the time, is less culpable than you or I right now going to picking up the phone and calling in a threat to the President. There is a qualitative difference in the level of -- of the offense between what Mr. Russell did that night in XXXX and a person perfectly sane, competent person making this call. And the guidelines don't take that into account.

So, in terms of Booker or 3553 factors, it seems to me that the nature of the offense and his situation at the time of the offense is--plays a huge part in whether or not -- in forming the sentence and forming a sentence that is lower than the guidelines, because the guidelines as such do not take into account this factor, and makes him very different than somebody else like you or I who would have been in this exact same guideline range doing the exact same conduct.

The other part of it is there's nothing in Mr. Russell's history that indicates that he's out to threaten the President or do any harm to the President. And if you put this in context as to what he saying, he's talking about being chased by dogs from Alabama, that people--some of the -- because of a book he's read -- because of a book he's written, and they're trying to keep it from being published and that the Secret Service agents are picking off people, killing people who are trying to kill him. You know, all of this is occurring in this great big delusional situation that's going on in his head. This is not someone who is planning to go out and get a gun or kill the President. I think that's acknowledged in the presentence report. This is someone who clearly is delusional.

He's now been on medication. He's not being forcibly medicated. He's voluntarily taking his medication. And he's a very different person. He-- you know, to talk to him now, he's lucid, he's not evidencing any of these kinds of delusions. He understands what's going on. I mean, he went through a plea hearing with Your Honor in which you could tell he was totally different person than what's been described in these psychological reports. Medication helps him.

Ms. One made an argument that, well, if he gets out he's going to decompensate and become dangerous again because there's nobody there to make sure he takes his medication. Well, it's very easy for the Court to make mental health counseling and compliance with his medication regime a condition of supervised release. He's going to be on supervised release. That gives the appropriate check on him and allows for -- for the monitoring and the continued good progress that he's been making.

He also has a place to go when he gets out. His mother runs an apartment complex in Florida. He's got--she's agreed to put him to work as a maintenance man there. He has a place to live. There are county mental health services available there. So he's got sort of family and the support ready to go there. All of these things, I think, put into place a situation where he would not be dangerous and the Court could have confidence that this is going to be a situation where he can go out, continue his medication, and not be--I mean, he's already not the person he was then and I think he can continue to be.

So we would ask the Court to impose a reasonable sentence, both as a downward departure or -- either as a downward departure or a Booker variance. And I also suggest that there are serious Eighth Amendment implications for sentencing somebody to higher sentence based on their mental illness. And I just have some concern about that as well. So, with all of that I would ask the Court to sentence him to 18 months.

THE COURT: All right.

MR. TWO: -- and be done with it.

THE COURT: Thank you, sir.

Mr. Russell, you have the right to address the Court personally and make any statement that might desire to make, and I'll give you that chance right now. You're not obligated to do so, but if you'd like to, you may.

MR. TWO: Judge, do you mind if he sits down?

THE COURT: He may sit right there is fine.

THE DEFENDANT: Well, Your Honor, when I left XXXX that -- I guess I'll start from the beginning, if you don't mind. I went up on a mountain and painted my face and I laid down on a rock and prayed to God for the children. And I did a ritual while I was there and I left down the mountain. Well, that night I woke up and -- by an angel that told me: My name is Mercy, I here -- I come and gave it and now I come to take it away. And these voices started talking to me. I never had voices talking to me. And, so, I listened to these voices, and things

-- people were chasing me and they were--I was listing to the voices. And they were trying to kill me, and actually the voices is actually told me to say -- to threaten the President because I would find safety.

And I'm not the same person anymore. I'm -- I've been through a lot in my life. I've made a lot of mistakes and I've grown. And during this period here, I've learned that the voices will lie to you. And I'm not hearing anymore because I'm taking my medication. And my mom, you know, has got a place for me, and I miss her. I miss my family. And, you know, myself, I just--it's been a long road, so.

THE COURT: Is that all, Mr. Russell?

THE DEFENDANT: Yes, sir.

THE COURT: All right. Thank you, sir.

Well, you know this is very unpleasant for everybody. I think it's a very unfortunate situation. The Government has acknowledged, and I think the defendant through his counsel acknowledged, that the defendant was suffering from psychotic episode at the time of the event in question. And Mr. Two, you've argued long and hard for compassion and mercy due to his status, and have even gone so far as to make legal arguments that certain punishments would be impermissible under out Constitution as amended because of his mental condition. But the problem is he's not going to be punished for his mental condition. That's the problem with your argument. And I must -- you know, my purpose in coming here today, and in reading this report very carefully, was to be just and apply the law and my judgment as impartially and objectively as I could. It was for that reason that I gave your client the benefit of doubt regarding the number of threats involved, and his sentence would be more severe but for me having done that.

But having said that, I think that he--I -- what it all boils down to, in summarizing the argument that Ms. One made, her argument could be captured succinctly by saying this was a serious and real threat regardless of his actual ability to carry it out or not. He certainly had a potential to carry it out. The question is: Is it really serious?

The defendant's argument, in essence, as I understand it, or at least one construction of that argument could be it really wasn't that serious because he was never going to do it. And it was all a -- it was a cry for help. It was admittedly the wrong thing to do and he's legally responsible, but it really isn't that serious for all of those reasons. And one of the arguments the defendant made was that the guidelines don't contemplate a situation like this.

Well, I -- you know, my response to that is that it's hard for me to believe that the Sentencing Commission, when crafting the guidelines, did not recognized the fact a substantial percentage of person who threaten the life of the President are mentally unstable. I think it would be probably said to be common knowledge of that fact. And, yet, the guidelines do not carve out an exception for circumstances such--as this. And on the whole, after considering all the evidence, I think that an appropriate sentence is at the high end of the guidelines and I'm going to sentence him to just that.

I'll sentence the defendant to 37 months.

And order him to pay the mandatory special assessment of $100.

I will not fine the defendant and will not order the defendant to pay any costs of incarceration.

Upon release from imprisonment, the defendant shall be placed on supervised release for a term of 3 years.

And within 72 hours of release from the custody of the Bureau of Prisons, the defendant shall report in person to the probation office in the district to which he is released.

During the 3 years the defendant is on supervised release, he shall not commit another federal, state, or local crime. And he shall comply with the standard conditions that have been adoped by this Court and the following additional conditions.

He shall not own, posses, or control any firearm, dangerous weapon, or other destructive device.

He shall participate in drug and alcohol treatment program as directed by the probation officer and, if able; contribute to the cost of those services.

He shall participate in a mental health treatment program under the guidance and supervision of the probation officer.

And he shall cooperate in the collection of DNA as directed by the probation officer.

He shall submit while on supervised release to a search of his person and property and residence, office, and/or vehicle at a reasonable time and in a reasonable manner based upon reasonable suspicion of contraband or evidence of violation of condition of release. And the failure to submit to a search may be grounds for revocation. And he shall warn other residents that the premises may be subject to searches pursuant to this condition.

The record should reflect that this recommendation takes into consideration the applicable sentencing factors under 18, U. S. C. Section 3553 (a). And I've carefully considered all of those factors and believe that this is fair and just and reasonable sentence under all circumstances.

Mr. Russell, you have 10 days to appeal my sentence. And you may do so filing a written notice of appeal in the Clerk's Office. If you fail to do that within 10 days, you would forever lose or waive your right to appeal in this case.

Do you understand that?

DEFENDANT: Yes, sir.

THE COURT: Okay. Are there any exceptions to the sentence?

MS. ONE: Not from the Government, Your Honor. Thank you.

MR. TWO: Judge, I would reiterate all of the exceptions that I made before both as to guidelines, particularly the 4-level reduction, the 3-level increase for the threat to the President, as well as the fact finding made along therewith.

Also, I would object to the Court's refusal to downwardly depart based on my arguments under the guidelines. Also, I would object because the sentence is both procedurally and substantively unreasonable. The Court has failed to adequately consider all the factors. I know the Court has just said that, but I want to make it for the record. The Court hasn't adequately considered all the factors.

I think the issue about not providing--not allowing me the opportunity to present the video is--renders the sentencing procedurally unreasonable as well as substantively unreasonable, and I believe that would be it.

THE COURT: All right. Thank you.

MR. TWO: Thank you.

End of Hearing! I lost my appeal.

= Chapter 11 =

I was clearly not in my right frame of mind the day of court. I did not know the things I know today, plus I was on heavy meds at the time. The whole court hearing was a shock, because the things said about me, was fare from the truth, I was floored. I broke down and cried at that hearing. My lawyer made a good argument but he too was not clear of the facts and couldn't defend me the way I should have been defended, he was my second lawyer, the first lawyer didn't lesson to the facts of what happen, that is stated in my first book Insanity. Nor did he know the facts.

I went to prison with the most dangers people in the U. S. , people who were not getting out, who had life sentences. I lived in fear and had nervures brake downs. I'm so thankful I'm a free man and thankful I can tell my side of all this, from the book Insanity to this follow up.

You have the chance to really see inside some hard times I went through. For a man to go to prison and know in his heart he didn't mean the crime held against him is hard. I write this book to have not just to have you know the truth, but those who punished me to know all the facts.

I have made plenty of mistakes in life and learned things the hard way, but this last punishment should have never happen. I will write a letter to George W. Bush, one of the best Presidents in my eyes, I like him from the very beginning. Yes, I said things and I explained why and how it came to that, but it will not rest in my soul tell he knows all the facts. After I went to prison they sent me to a halfway house that I did not go to, I went to the hospital, they charged me with escape and I did more time for it, all in all I did 44 months.

Can one ever say that he is a changed man and know in his heart that he has grown, the answer is yes. From my troubled young to life in prison as a man I have grown to be thankful. I can't go back and changed my mistakes but I can make it clear that some things were done in fain.

For the judge I have no hard feelings, because if I were in his shoes I too would have looked at it the way he did, because just look how it was laid out for him. Now let me move forward and let the reader see what else I bring to the table.

There have been things said while I was out of my mind, but now that I'm clearly laying out the facts I want to express one last letter concerning what you just examined. I can only hope that this will be taken to the next level in the heart of the ones I hurt for bringing the shame on my life and the ones around me that the door will close and everyone will know the truth.

This letter I'm about to write will be given as a token to the days I spent thinking did the President ever read letters I sent him. As this book is published and Mr. Bush reads it I hope he looks back in his files and see the many letters I sent trying to tell him my true feelings. This is not going to be like the so many I wrote before but things I want to lay out for the record.

Here is a letter to George W. Bush out President, from the man who spent so many years in prison for saying a threat that should never have been said, and this is what I have to say to him.

Dear President George W. Bush,

Greetings! May this letter find you well and in the best of spirits. I wrote you many letters when you where in office, sent them to the White House. I know you most likely never read them because of all the mail you received while in office, but if you have record of them I hope you still have access to them. From the very beginning I wanted you to know that I never mint you any harm and I tried my best to explain, even while I was not mentally stable.

The things I want to say in this letter is history and things you may know, but feel the need to be said. First of all I want to say sorry for what happen and hope you can find in your heart to forgive me. I think you did a really good job in office. As I write this in all merit I hope you understand my claim as well as except my apology.

Mr. Bush I want to bring up a few things. Project MK-ULTRA was the code name for a covert, illegal CIA human research program. The program began in the 1950's, it was sup post to have stop in the 1970's and the files destroyed in 1973 of those who where involved, they manipulated individual mental states and alter brain functions. There was also Operation Paperclip that the recruits were former Nazi scientist. Some of the scientist studied torture and brainwashing. Several secret U. S. government projects grew out of Operation Paperclip. Experiments were often conducted without the subject knowledge. CIA documents show that "radiological, biological, and chemicals used for that purpose of mind control as part of MK-ULTRA. That took place on people, its apart of history, and I feel I went through some sort of covert operation that lead me to say the threat against you. As you know one of the main areas investigated by the CIA was mind control.

I'm sure you know Wilelm Reich was an Austrian American psychiatrist. He lived in Germany when Adolf Hitler came to power in 1933, he moved to the U. S. in 1939. In December 1944 Reich began series of bion experiments. In 1940, Reich wrote to Albert Einsten saying he had a scientific discovery he wanted to discuss, and 1941 went and visited Einsten.

In December 1941 Reich was arrested by the FBI and questioned about several books found in his home. Reich was released in 1942, but in 1957 he was put into prison, were he died. Reich was a well known scientist; he created an electrical box that could manipulate one's mind without them knowing it. All his books were studied by our government.

My point is that our brain is a electrical receiver, and can be electrically touched by passing the ear, and I'm sure you know a great deal of Psychological Warfare, it being real in foreign countries as well as ours. Science has come a long way since Wihelm Reich, even though he had invented how to do such, and that electrical box was used.

Not long ago I saw in a science magazine the smallest radio in the world, it could only be seen by a magnify glass, it was that small, and it was on the market.

I believe now it was a military Sy-Ops affair that made me hear voices. At the time I thought it was Gods voice. When I was involved the War on Terrist I believe I was placed with an RFID chip, or some sort of chip that is still embedded in my body. In my left butt cheek, under the skin is a piece of medal. If you read my first book you would know I lived inside the mafia. I had what I thought was a bug bite on my butt cheek, but it's now clear a piece of medal is under the skin, getting a doctor to remove it is a challenge. One day it will be removed.

Mr. President, people like Black Water have high Tec intelligence. If it was not our government who used electrical War Fare, it was someone who has the knowhow. I was entrapped to say the things I said about you. I wish I could take the things I said back, because I truly didn't mean what the voices told me to say. If someone hears a voice they think it's a higher power, and Sir, now all that I said came about you came from that voice along with what I explained in my first book.

The time I spend in prison was hell on earth. It took a long time to heal and I lost years because of all that happen. If you know in your heart that I never mint you any harm than I can live with the past better. I know people serve this country over sea and here, and my prayers go out to them. There have been times I prayed for you. This country is the best on earth, but it's not perfect. May you be blessed and God Bless our country.

Mr. President, may the truth be known. I never mint you any harm!

Sincerely,

Jeremiah Russell

2011

= Chapter 12 =

Here is what lead up to all this.

The experience I'm about to tell you are some of the wildest things that anyone has ever gone through. I write this later because I've been in prison. I will explain how I landed in prison and all the events that have exploded my life. I will start by where I left off. There are a few copies floating around parts of my book though. Good luck.

The story was more than chance, but an unusual theme. I remember how it lay out like a story from the inscription of my mind. Here I want to travel back to Venice Florida. I was living with a woman, the love of my life. She had a young daughter. I have spoken about them earlier in my first book Insanity, and I'm sure that you remember the night I woke up after being sexually assaulted. I didn't know what happened just that something had happened. My tail hurt. There was blood in the number two that I did when I first woke up in the middle of the night. A few days later, I find out the little girls dad had come over and stuck a stick in my ass. The reader should be aware these pages are sobering as most of the writings are. The girlfriend did betray me. I wanted to kill him and her, but he lived where I didn't a clue as to where it was. She was sworn nothing had happened.

To tell these stories, I've got to go back to those scars I have and I've tried to heal. The event was torture on my heart. My main goal was to find out the facts of what had taken place. My girlfriend which I call her by the name of flower was a powerful woman. Her love for me was deeper than I ever gone, but to explain her would be something more than a devotion but mere love. I could not get the truth from her and I chose to leave her. One can only take something like that one or two ways and I chose to contact the law secretly. They did nothing but contact child custody people because the little girl had said that statement to me and also told me something had happened to her by her dad.

The hurt of this story is almost over for the reader but I live on with what happened. Once I left, she came to win me back after a few days gone living on the streets. I know that sounds foolish that I went back to her, but it was more to our love than meets the eye, plus I was on skid row

Flower was involved with a lot of people. She was sexy and had a way about her that was irresistible. She made me her lover. She wanted me close by at all times. She had me on watch from people around town. She knew I was in a trap in her circle. Flower told me if I ever left her, she would have killed me. She claimed she could have anyone killed and had them killed already.

I slept with one eye open and armed. Finally, I couldn't take it anymore and I couldn't get close enough to get my revenge on the baby's daddy, where Flower had set me up. I knew a lot about her circle of people and she knew I knew things. After the child custody people came, she had made it clear I was in big trouble. I went to the streets of Sarasota, Florida and had left her again.

As I rode the public bus, I saw Flowers circle of people riding up to Sarasota ahead of the bus and that alarmed me because that was how I lived; it was my instinct which were right most of the time. The bus ride took over forty minutes. I remember it storming really hard on the way there. Once I got there, it had stopped raining. The place I went to was the Sarasota library. I got online and asked for some prayers about the trouble I was in and then I walked to the Salvation Army. Inside the place, I took a shower at times, so I took one and then lay on a mat to get some rest afterwards. There were people talking about the circle of people of Flowers and I felt in danger from them by the things they were saying secretly. I got up from the mat and left.

There was a place I would sleep through over the years off and on, when I was on skid row, on top of a church roof. On my way there, about a two mile walk, I noticed a helicopter in the sky. The years I lived there, I couldn't remember ever seeing a helicopter flying around the city. It was way up in the sky. As I went around the side streets, I then noticed a car following me with a group of people in it. I then noticed another car following me, and then I could tell that there were three cars circling.

I would dip from street to street. I finally went down by the rail road tracks and out I came near where I had planned to go. Still watching the helicopter, knowing it was odd for it to be up there. I went around the back of the building and it already had become dark out by this time. Now, I know I've told you things supernatural that had happened to me, but I'll tell you this, there was the sound of frogs making the sounds of goats. I found that to be amazing because it sounded just like a goat. It took me a second to figure out it was a frog. They were out because it had rained.

Since it was wet out, I didn't climb up on the top of the church roof, but instead found a foxhole, a hiding place under a leaning piece of ply wood, next to the side of the building. I have lived skid row off and on for years but that night, I was very alert of all that was going on. I fell asleep. I had to be awoken by the helicopter hovering just right over me. I came out of my hiding place and when I did the helicopter flew off.

I walked around to the front of the building. I was standing there when I saw a black guy walking across the street in my direction. It didn't take me long to notice he had a pistol under his shirt. As he walked across the street at me, I walked across staying about thirty yards away. He was eye balling me and it only made me keep more distance. I walked over into the IHOP parking lot and there were people inside. I didn't yell gun but more or less, I watched the guy. He watched me as well. Finally he went between the buildings and disappeared.

The cars that had been following me earlier, one that I had spotted circling was out circling the streets. I hid behind the IHOP for awhile. I knew Flower had a hit out on me.

About a half hour later, I started walking to a new place. There was a lot of people down the road. I crossed the road to avoid them. The odd thing was as I passed they called for me. I yelled back 'I'm busy" and kept moving. As I got across the group and down the road I made my way down by the police station. There was a phone across the street. I had left my cell phone at Flowers because of the GPS system on it. It was early in the morning, about 2 AM or so. I called Flower and she answered. I told her to call off the hit on me, that I would come back and that I loved her. I could tell someone was there with her. She had ties with the gang network in Sarasota, but she lived in Venice.

Flower never would confess to anything. It was part of her ways. I found a place to rash next to the police station and oddly they came out the back and yelled, "Good Morning Vietnam!" I was well known in Sarasota and I got the message the law knew I was in trouble. The next day I was back with Flower and her little beautiful daughter that I cared for as much as I loved anything ever.

Things at flowers were different after the assault. I drank out of cans and never left the one open were I couldn't see it. I stopped drinking beer and me and Flower drank crown royal and coke. We did love each other but she is a tough woman. As I set here in this prison cell writing three years later, I haven't heard from her since my prison arrest. I'll get into how I got here and things. One morning a few weeks, maybe about a month later, I still lived in fear. I was drugged and I thought the worst after the sexual assault. I wondered if there were pictures of some sort, but that morning, I had to flee again. I had gone to work and had a cup of coffee before leaving. My chest started hurting badly. I had been hurting for about an hour at work when I said to the guy I was working with that I needed to go home. I left work, went to Flowers and called a friend who advised me to get out of there.

I packed my stuff and got on a grey hound bus. I went to Anniston, Alabama. My chest hurt for two weeks. I don't know what happened but I think someone put something in my coffee. When I arrived in Anniston, I went to eth Salvation Army. There was a guy who showed up that day who told me to keep a low profile. He told me there were people from Venice and said it had to do with politicians. I used the Anniston library to go to the web and told people what was up and how they had someone there from Venice. I unloaded all I knew and knew I was still in danger.

I got a job with an uncle and was staying at his house. He was remodeling. Anniston has a military base there and some of the stuff I emailed dealt with military stuff. The first person, who approached me at my new hide out, my uncles' house, was a military guy. He talked in circles, but I heard all I had to hear to know he knew some of the stuff

69

I emailed. I was unwilling to talk to him and our meeting was brief in the front yard.

The next events are hard to conceive but not only super natural but military warfare. I start off by how it all went down to finally getting arrested. The day before Halloween I painted my face and went walking to where my family lived on the mountain side. I stopped and bought a bible, I already was feeling weird with my subconscious thoughts, so I bought two cans of sardines and a cigar. I walked up the mountain to a big rock and did some praying, crying, and a few spiritual things.

I know the military has satellites that can zoom down and see things and I at the time thought all what was happening was from God, but now I've learned that military caused it as well. I came down the mountain; my face cleared and then walked the five miles back to the house I was remodeling. That night I had a spiritual phoneme. Today, I can only testy to what happened, but can't say how it was done. I lost all normal reality. I will explain. As I lay in the floor, I woke out of sleep and started uttering very fast. Voices started to speak through me, not my voice but others. It was more than five voices speaking all sounding different, talking to one another. As I went into this trance, listening as I was uttering, another voice spoke through me.

There was a radio in the house, a boom box the people on the radio was asking questions and I had become a voice radio as I uttered. This went on a few days. I was alone at the house. I couldn't control the voices I uttered but when I uttered I could only listen to what my tongue was saying. I know this is very strange.

The stuff I knew of the military was being questioned over the radio boom box. One night I was laying on the floor asleep and was awoken by an angle who said, "My name is Mercy. I came and gave it, now I come to take it away. "

Three years later, in prison I tell you that I told the truth. I'm finally able to write about this because time now has become the right time. I've learned so much and I'll tell you about it. This house wasn't home for long. The neighbors knew something was going on there. I was under radar as well. The next door neighbor had always ha d a few people out in the yard at night and I was indie my uncles house making noises. There was one night a few nights into his crazy trip one foot the voices told me to get out of the house that were people going to challenge me. I was crazy as one could be, but really listened close to all the voices were saying. I spent a lot of time uttering. I was amazed.

That night, I fear I opened the back window because the voice told me to get out. They were in front of the house. Well, I went out the window and moments later there were gun shots, three of them. I ran down the road to a building and was hiding there when a voice in my head told me they were after me. They would find me there, so I waited a second and started through the woods. I got into a water drain hole that went into the side of a hill. The voice in my head was clear, a telepath. Before the reader says I'm crazy, Google MK – ultra CIA. They can radio you and by pass your ear.

As I got deep into the pipe the voice said, "Be very quiet, because they are about to shoot the gunman," and seconds later I heard a gunshot over the top of where I was. Now the ones who have read the book "Insanity" will understand why I have people wanting to hurt me. It's not just Flower or the Mafia, I've pissed off the satanic cult, and the few copies that first went out underground the cult got a copy. The cult is very large.

Okay, after the gun shot the voice told me in my head to wait, then it told me to come out, and that they had killed the gunman, there was a gunshot and I came out. I fled on foot; I left all of my stuff, my wallet, my money, and my new cell phone. I planned to go to my hometown in Georgia and find a job. I made my escape again, it was clear they had found me. On food, I went and called the law, which called one of m family members. The law said, "What do you think we can do about it?" My family said I was crazy.

On my two feet, I went walking, uttering, and listening to those voices. I had gone crazy but I was very sane. I wouldn't' utter in front of people. I hitchhiked to Georgia. I was going to walk but people kept giving me rides.

In Atlanta, I got on a bus to Marietta which was only a few miles up the raod. The bus driver gave me the ride for free. I went to the shelter to eat. The voices in my head were there and when I uttered the voices kept telling me to do thins. I left the shelte rafter eating and walking down the raod. I was headed to Cherokee County. The voice told me to go into the woods, and I did as I was told. They told me to hurry and hide, they were coming after me! Just a few moments later there were three gun shots right above the embankment. It sounded as if someone fell from a tree.

I was scared as hell hiding on the side of the bushes. There was another shot fired not far off. I stayed hidden. After about five minutes the voice told me to tell the other people that were there to leave. The voices were like telepathy. I used my telepathy and told them I could hear people scaling down the trees, five minutes later It said to leave and that the police were on their way. I went through the woods and come out the back part of the woods, where there was a side street. An undercover car was coming down the back street and swerved at me and kept going.

I slept outside that night for a few minutes until I was awakened by a voice that said that they had found me again. I walked and crossed the highway and down a street. There was a car with its emergency lights on. The voice said, "They were looking for me. " It still being night I walked away from there but they came running at me. I ran and ran through yards and the voice was making me panic.

I jumped on a side off an embankment and laid there. I heard footsteps running up behind me but they stopped next to someone's back yard storage building. I was frozen and the voice told me to be very still because they were there. People were looking for me. Ten minutes later, I saw big rats crawling on me . I didn't want to be bitten nor did I want to be found, so the rats were all over me till I jumped up and rolled down the hill. I yelled out, "don't move police!" because that is what came out. Now, you got to remember when I spoke that there was more than just me that I could utter.

That night, I made a lot of ground. The sun came up and I went to the paint store. I had a rip in my camouflage pants leg. I was in camouflage because I had my ever hunting license before all of this. I had a bow and arrow ready for the season. This took place in November. That day, I tried to find old friends I had worked for at the paint store. By the afternoon I was fleeing again through the woods. I jumped fences, I jumped creeks, and the voices let me know when they were close. Plus, I could hear the stuff in the woods. I was on no drugs, but really tripping.

One close encounter was when I was running in to barn after a hundred yard dash. Someone saw me running into the barn. I was at someone house in the back yard. After holding in there for about an hour a police officer opened the door. I ran because I was in fear. Well as I went through the woods again it was night time by this time and there were dogs out, they sounded as though they were after me. I ran and got stuck in a bunch of weeds and briars. At times I had to crawl on my hands and needs.

= CHAPTER 13 =

The dogs were getting closer on my trial and the voice said to climb a tree. Dogs had to get so close so I did. I prayed for God to help me and it started raining so the dogs lost the trail. The voice said they had found me right there in the tree. I yelled from the tree. I came down the tree, laid in the wet cold ground. The voice said to be very still. I plead my case not to kill me that I was royal ranger and people were out there to help me. After five minutes they were gone. I went again through the woods. I found myself up on top of someone's shed. A tin roof and the people who lived there were under it with a gun about three in the morning. They never said anything but I could hear them moving around and the voice said they had a gun.

I'm out in the middle of nowhere on this tin shed. The voice said to be very quiet. They finally threw a rock up on top by me almost hitting me. That's when I knew I better plead my case. I told them I was unarmed and people were on their way to help me. About ten minutes later the voice in my head said to come.

I was deep into the woods getting cut up by the brush. I had scratches on my face. I was cold and wet. Someone shot a gun over a hill side where I just was. The reader can tell this was all unnatural as hell and a wild ass time I had. The next morning I started raining again. I walked into a church and asked the preacher if I could get a bite to eat. He said, "sir, if you died today, where would you go?" I told him hell and said a few off the wall things, but he gave me two sandwiches and it was like salvation to be able to move on. I didn't want to talk about anything with him, and he didn't act like he wanted to know why I was soaking wet in the cold.

I went up the road and slept a few hours. Now the night before I was running along the trails of deer prints in the mud and that day I saw a deer on the side of the road that had been hit by a car. I wondered if it was the deer that left those prints. Not likely because there are a lot of deer around there. Still, I wondered.

As I got up the road I came to a gas station. I wanted more to eat but had no money because my wallet was in Alabama. The voice was clear as day in my head and it said, to get to a pay phone and threaten the president. It said I would get help and the federal government would give me a hearing on all the troubles I had. I ran far enough. I got to a pay phone and said, "My name is Jeremiah Russell. I want to kill the president. I'm down at this store, come and get me. "

The impact of my imagination and facts were side by side. This spiritual guide has brought me along way. There is no doubt that the government was using MK-Ultra or some other mind control device. At the time I had no clue as to what and how it could have been done.

When the officer showed up, I came from behind the store. There was a man who had come back behind there to smoke some weed and offered me some. I had quite months earlier. I walked over to the police car and said, "I'm the one you're looking for. " He placed me under arrest and at that time I was very confused. I wanted to get out of the cold rain and therefore I didn't go into a lot with the officer. He took me to the precinct. There was not telling how many people were looking for me but I knew I was now safe. At the precinct two secret service men showed up. I felt as though they knew about me. I told them all of what was doing on except about the voices, but I went into trying to explain the events that I went through the last three days.

I was confused on how I would get help from them, but after a few minutes they wanted to take me to another place. The two officers took me to a hospital and then sent me to another hospital that refused to take me. The officers followed an ambulance that they placed me in. I had been confirmed as crazy and head to another hospital.

Not only was I receiving electrical forces in my mind, I also had a good sense of smell. There was not a day without voices I uttered told me the CI A was going to try and kill me. Someone from there did come visit me. I had never heard voices nor had I ever been able o utter. The other voice speaking was all new to me, but that was happen and it was interesting to me. It was geared into full force. Those voices spoke about all kinds of things and some of the voices I knew were of other people I knew. It sounded like their voices. The voices told me to cover my mouth and then the air condition would come on. The voices would tell things before It would happen, like someone was about to come to the door and all kinds of things.

The voice told me the CIA was putting gas in the AC and I noticed people in other rooms were coughing. I would cover my mouth with a rag. As I give this testimony I hope the reader comes to find this as madness, because it was. I over came these microwave systems and methods that were being done by the military.

The story goes on. As I was in the hospital the staff and patients were being called from the outside. the people who were after me did a good job of find me. This time a patient informed that there was a Russian mafia calling in and asking about me. My life was under air conditional operation that threatened my life. It could have been the CIA. Now I knew people had found me at the hospital. My anxiety and life had become crazy. I had in the past informed on the 9-11 world trade center stuff as I lived in Venice where they trained. Some of the stuff I wrote right before was the start of the spiritual madness in my head. Now I was under a spiritual attack that I had no chance to control.

I don't think it's legal to do someone like they did to me. I made enemies with the wrong people I guess the government as involved. I still have questions of who and why. The federal marshals came and picked me up and took me to court. They had me heavily medicated that day. Normally I would check the drugs and flush them. But the night before I went off and flipped the pill car and they shot me with a needle. I went off because the voice told me that night the others patients were going to hurt me. Now this voice would tell me the truth some I believed it. The other times it would lie.

Well after court, I was sent to a place in South Carolina hen after a few days I was flown to Springfield, Missouri. I had stopped uttering the last few weeks at that time because of the threat at the last hospital. I continued to check my medication, but if I started uttering I would have been force medicated. I never did my uttering in front of people, just when I was alone. By this time, I landed in Springfield prison, I was unsure of how it would go.

I would get these high pitched ringing in my left ear. The uttering was supernatural and there were seven different voices. Unbelievable, I know. Now this testimony is true and maybe hard to believe, but if you believe anything I've said you will know I was tripping. When I t would rain and storm I would utter and would say the word lightening and right that second lightening strike would go through the sky. It did this off and on. I wanted to know more about the government MK-Ultra electronical warfare, but after all I've gone through, I know God is still the holder of the keys to all of these phenomena.

Well I went to court and everyone said I was crazy. It didn't stop them from not caring at court about my charge. I didn't want to take the painful drugs they wanted me to take. They forced them on me and sentenced me to three years in prison for the phone call. I went through prison time without much trouble and was released to go to a half way house. I had pleaded for protection in my letters as I knew the danger would still be out there once I got out. I got on a greyhound bus headed for the halfway house. I saw someone I assumed following me. I didn't know if I was over fearful or that my life was still in danger. I didn't go to the halfway house. I had to do more time because of that in the worst prison holding center.

As my spiritual life has grown to be at peace, I've mastered myself and have overcome the uttering. I do plenty of mediation and prayer. After all I've been through, I feel I'm much wiser than most people . I feel God has forgiven me for some of things I've written and said. I put myself in a spiritual pickle. I believe I can overcome the enemy, I overcome the electrical assaults. It's hard for me to believe my country did this to me. I know the Russians could have done some of those electrical phenomena. Electrical fields are high tech stuff, but I also know God played a part in all some of it. I now am a free man and healed. My life will never be the same.

The end,

Jeremiah Russell